With special thanks to:

Darron and my beautiful children,
for still being by my side,

Mum and Dad, a constant in everything,

Grandma who helped us 'hang in there',

Fiog, Katy, Sue and Skip, very special friends
whose support carried me through

and

Pauline and Val, gurus of all things literary.

There are so many people that have helped me on this
journey, not all can be listed here but I am just so glad that in
the end we made it through together, none of you are
forgotten, especially Steve.

I hope you all know what you mean to me.

While this memoir is a work of non-fiction, some characters names have been changed to protect those involved.

INTRODUCTION

In the early days of 2004 our world would be turned on its axis and instead of welcoming our new baby we would be left accused of shaking him and fighting to keep both our children in the legal battle of a lifetime.

The long two year struggle through the Family Court and subsequent five year journey, filled with a roller-coaster of health scares and moments of self-doubt, would eventually lead us to the true cause of my youngest son's brain haemorrhage. The reason why we had been ordered to move out of our own home and spend every hour, sick with worry, came as suddenly as the accusations themselves had done. It was then we realised that if it could be us, it could be anyone.

We do not seek to apportion blame on anyone, we do not seek retribution, we seek the truth - for all.

When secrecy replaces confidentiality, when 'justice' can no longer be justified, when the system fails to protect and instead abuses and when doctors are asked to diagnose causes and not conditions, that is when truth no longer matters.

Join the 24:14 campaign at:

www.searchfortruth.co.uk

What is 24:14?

- **A nationwide protocol** for all hospitals to help doctors differentiate between child abuse and non-abuse (Potential to go global)

- 24:14 ensures that all babies/children are seen by Paediatric specialists within 24 hours of admission

- Reviewed up to 14 days later

- 24:14 prevents cases like **'Baby P'** (MISSED FOR ABUSE) and **Angela Cannings** (WRONGLY ACCUSED OF ABUSE)

- It would take £2 million for a pilot of 24:14, which equates to 0.2% of £1 billion pound cost of child abuse to statutory and voluntary agencies.

When Truth No Longer Matters

By

Heather Toomey

CHAPTER 1.

The room is dark as I try to focus my eyes and understand what my ears are hearing. In the gloom I can just make out the figure of my eight year old son Mark, who is upset but not crying. I reach for the touch lamp at the side of the bed and tap it with rather more force than is actually required and leaning up on one arm, my son's face comes into view.

Mark is not overly tall for his age, blocky in build but slim, his face is blotchy and panic stricken, he has obviously been working himself up to waking me, as he tells me that Sean is making funny noises. It is 5.00a.m.in the morning and as my husband Darron ambles to the bathroom he calls "He's probably snoring", as I get out of bed to investigate.

Two things immediately strike me as odd; of my two boys it would be Mark who would normally snore lightly, he is the one whose covers are normally sliding off at all angles, his body contorted into amazing shapes that he would probably struggle to make in his waking hours. Sean on the other hand, younger, smaller and even more slight than his brother, sleeps exactly as you leave him. He makes his bed dutifully every morning by flipping over the corner he has just got out of, his many cuddly friends perched across the top of his bed hardly move save for 'sheepy', a very round circular soft toy with tiny ears and legs that takes up more room in the bed than Sean does.

The second unusual thing is the distressed state of Mark, who, intelligent and hard working, is not usually one for dramatics or emotional outbursts; he is exact in his nature and sensible to the very core. With every fibre of my being I know something is wrong.

Mark and Sean have long since shared a bedroom at their own request. When they had first decided to sleep in the same room I put an airbed on the floor, sure that within a matter of a day or two the novelty would have worn off and they would be back in their own beds. After a couple of months I had to give in and move both beds into the same room, where they have stayed ever since. We have frequently been woken by the giggles and shrieks of laughter coming from the room next to ours, usually at an ungodly hour, far too early to be reasonable.

They revel in each other's company and, although they have the usual brotherly squabbles, by the time I try to intervene they look at me innocently and declare nothing is wrong. This prompts me to try and put on my most serious 'tell me the truth' look before merely getting a grin from Mark causing Sean to laugh loudly.

This morning there was no laughter as I entered the children's bedroom. The room, darker than ours due to the blackout curtains we bought in a vain attempt to encourage a later wake-up call, was lit only by Mark's bedside lamp, casting shadows across the carpeted floor. The noise Mark was describing was unusual and, as I approached Sean's bed, I called to him but got no response. I turned on the bedside light to discover him twitching uncontrollably, the left side of his body drooped and his left eye turned downwards. I called his name again but his focus never moved, his eyes staring as his eyelids fluttered incessantly. In a re-run of a situation I had been in years before, I yell Darron, who is making his way out of the bathroom. "Dial 999, call an ambulance!"

Darron comes into the room out of a need to know what is going on but I don't give him chance to find out as I shriek the instruction again. He stalls for a split second before running for the phone on the landing and, having dialled, comes back to me wanting answers, asking uncertainly what is going on.

I hear Darron relay our address prior to thrusting the phone in my direction. As Sean vomits repeatedly, I beg the operator to hurry and I am reassured that the ambulance is already well on its way. Darron now waits anxiously outside for the ambulance as I grab a flannel and rinse it with cold water in a bid to take Sean's temperature down. There is really no need, his forehead is not hot and his skin is waxy and white. "Not again" I think to myself, "please God not again".

I hear the paramedics climb the stairs and hear Darron tell Mark to wait in the living room. It is a sensible thing to do, we don't need any more bodies in the bedroom and the scene is one of chaos. The paramedics glean as much information as we can give them, listening attentively as they assess Sean, whilst simultaneously taking equipment out of their bags.

I imagine Mark waiting on the sofa downstairs, probably fussing the dog, who loves attention whatever the time of day. I realise how isolated Mark must feel and I go downstairs to hug him and bring him back with me as they finally succeed in getting a canula into the back of Sean's hand. I try my best to explain the situation to Mark and to reassure him. One of the paramedics does the same. I want him to know that it will all be alright, the seizure is stopping and we will soon be on our way to hospital.

We all get dressed quickly and, remembering how hot hospitals are, I dress sparsely for the February morning, before following Darron downstairs, as he carries Sean through the snow to the ambulance. I walk towards the front door and past where Mark is standing, staring after his brother and I pause, bending down and look straight into his eyes, I thank him for helping to save his brother.

—

It is then, overcome with emotion, that he starts to cry as he tells me he didn't do anything except to wake us up. I reply that it was enough and that we are lucky to have him.

Whilst hugging him tightly I tell him I am proud of him, reiterating that Sean will see him soon, before heading out of the door to where the ambulance is parked, its blue lights seeming even brighter in the darkness.

I clamber into the ambulance, reminded of a previous journey with Sean, but I do not worry whether I am doing the right thing. Sean needs medical care and the sooner he gets to the hospital the better. His face appears lopsided and I wonder if my little boy will ever look like himself again as he sleeps, exhausted. I have no idea what has caused the seizure as I hold his tiny hand, which seems to have shrunk, and put 'Sheepy' next to him. The paramedics are friendly and reassuring, but despite their jovial demeanour I can tell they are watching him closely and I feel eternally grateful for their support.

Even in the ambulance, with the sirens on and the lights flashing, it takes over half an hour to reach the hospital. The journey seems to go on longer, as I am unable to get my bearings through the small back windows, the lights inside preventing me seeing out.

As we pull up in accident and emergency Sean is wheeled straight through to resuscitation, as doctors and nurses take information, firstly from the paramedics and then from me.

I repeat all I know, which is very little, and trust that they will know more. His body looks tiny next to that of the older gentlemen in the next bay, whose wife looks at me sympathetically.

As doctors come in and out, I hover around Sean's bed. We aren't on a ward; there are no bedside televisions or jugs of water, only oxygen masks and beeping machines. The staff bustle around in a purposeful manner and the doctors return regularly, checking that Sean's breathing has returned to normal.

We have no idea how long Sean had been fitting before Mark was woken by what he later described as a choking noise with odd gurgles. All we knew was that the paramedic had taken ten minutes to stop the fit by administering doses of diazepam and it had taken at least that long for the ambulance to reach us from our placing the call.

I knew that it was serious. Sean, pale and washed out, isn't responsive, occasionally moaning but unable to talk. He isn't the bouncy, fun-loving boy who normally wakes us in the mornings and I am scared that something has changed and that the boy I know has gone.

Suddenly, without any prior movement or noise, Sean groans loudly, sits bolt upright in bed and then throws up all over the place. He is sick continually for several minutes before looking at me imploringly and saying "Mummy." My heart pounds as I realise he is still my Sean, he is still the same boy I had tucked in the previous night and he's going to be alright. Almost as suddenly as he had awoken he flops back on the bed and falls asleep again. I don't blame him and I don't care, I know he is OK and he will recover.

CHAPTER 2.

By the time Darron has parked the car and made his way to us we are preparing to leave for the ward. The nurse kindly offers us some toast and a drink, knowing that we had left home in a rush. It is now nearly 9.00a.m. and the hospital is becoming much busier as the day staff arrive. I can't face eating a thing, feeling anxious and sick I accept a cup of tea but decline the offer of toast. Darron, always a stress eater, eagerly munches his way through a slice before we are instructed to follow Sean up to the ward.

The surroundings on the ward are different; animated characters adorn the walls, jazzy patterned curtains, that you would never pick in a million years, hang around each bed. The sound of children playing echoes from the playroom next to the unit and the clatter of the breakfast trolley becomes louder as it comes into view.

The smiling lady manning the trolley is the sort of person who would have matched Sean perfectly. Positivity radiated from her as she greeted us cheerily asking what Sean might like for breakfast. Darron and I look at each other, as if the question is somehow a trick, Sean has spent the whole of the previous hour being sick and surely won't be hungry but a little voice from the bed tells us otherwise. Sean, who had only managed a few words that didn't make any sense but were encouraging all the same, responded with "Can I have some toast?" The lady, delighted in having an uptake on her offer, gives him an orange juice and goes to fetch the toast.

Darron and I chat to him animatedly, trying to sound casual and feeling very relieved. The toast arrives quickly and the lady hums as she pushes the trolley off the ward, waving bye-bye and declaring she would be back if he needed anything. Sean nibbles slowly, keen to eat but still very shaky.

He has eaten only a few mouthfuls when he declares he feels sick and proceeds to vomit again, and for the first time that morning Darron and I smile. Sean is always declaring he is hungry and it was cheering to know that today was no exception. He looks longingly at the rest of the toast but thinks better of it as he sips the orange and rests back on the bed. His head barely hits the pillow when a number of people come on to the ward and up to his bedside.

I guess that at least one of them is a doctor judging by the stethoscope and I recognise the distinctive blue nurses' uniforms but there are two more people who hang back cautiously. This deputation takes me by surprise, as the doctor at the front asks us to go over the morning in detail and asks permission for two students to be present. I smile at the two people who linger behind the doctor and nod in agreement and, as I do so, they move closer.

I go over everything in as much detail as I can recall and, although embarrassed, I do my best to mimic the seizure at the doctors' request. This visit is followed by regular checks from the nurses and additional requests for information from the doctors as they check on details and look up Sean's extensive and complex medical history.

Darron and I chat about nothing in particular; we have both been in a similar situation before and we have no desire to be here again. The old wounds run deep and the worry eats away at us as we wait for news. Our response to any questions is guarded and thought through as the doctors eventually file back on to the ward and the question we have been waiting for is asked.

They have read in Sean's history that as a tiny baby he had suffered a brain haemorrhage, to be exact a subdural haematoma, and they want to know what happened. It is the same question Darron and I have been asked a hundred times or more and the answer remains the same - we don't know!

I go through my medical history and the difficulties Sean had as a baby, as the paediatrician and student doctors listen to my every word. They interrupt only to clarify points before encouraging me to continue.

To my astonishment I only feel relief talking openly about it. Darron and I knew that there was no way they could help Sean without all the facts and I give them as much information as I have, but the truth is that on Sean's medical files the bleed on the inside of his brain is listed as non-accidental. It has no medical cause attributed to it because they could find no medical reason as to why he would have such a catastrophic injury, and because, after they raised the idea of a deliberate shaking injury, they had simply stopped looking.

As I recant the full details of Sean's history the doctors ask interested and relevant questions. For the first time I start to see that the doctors are considering the possibility that there may have been a mistake. We have no longer had any Social Services contact, except for the yearly Christmas card from our now retired social worker, in the last four years and this fact alone causes the medical professionals before us to consider what six years previously we had maintained: Sean's brain injury was not our fault.

As Sean was moved on to the ward, Darron and I discuss what should happen next and decide that I will stay at the hospital for the remainder of the day so that I could continue to provide doctors with any information needed. As Sean's mother it had been me who had been the one who was most involved with the many appointments he had attended and it made more sense for Darron to go home and pack some things for Sean and himself so that he could take over at night.

Throughout the remainder of the day, after Darron leaves, there are a steady stream of doctors and nurses to see

Sean. The number of interested students grows hourly and, with my medical notes to keep them going, there was plenty of background reading to go round!

The students are always tentative in their approach and sometimes apologetic for the disturbance, but as Sean is mostly sleeping I find their company comforting and their manner friendly. By late afternoon Sean is becoming much more like his old self. The temporary paralysis, which I had been informed was named 'Todd's Paresis', had gone and Sean's face was back to normal, his round eyes staring and blinking constantly because we had forgotten to pick up his glasses.

Sean had started to chat to the doctors himself, entertaining them as only he can and revelling in the attention. Only the events of that morning could have kept him in that bed, normally his dancing and singing is practically unavoidable, but today his manner is quieter but no less engaging. I have gone through all of Sean's medical history and the previous 'jitteriness' and tremors that he had shown as a baby and toddler and the recent strange vacantness that sometimes he demonstrated momentarily, only to pass so fast you weren't sure if it had happened or not. His bright and lively character was shining through and as they took blood samples and carried out tests he simply said "Ouch!" and furrowed his brow in a disapproving fashion.

Sean is small in height for his age and slight in build owing to the fact that bedtime is the only time he stops moving. People who don't know him often marvel at how much food he can eat, only to be truly shocked when he sucks his tummy in so far it looks concave, causing him to grin, knowing that he has caused a reaction.

There is, however, another side to Sean too - his heart is as big as he is. Ever since he was a very small baby his eyes would follow you around the room and you would get the feeling you were being watched. As he grew he would stare until he caught your eye and then smile a beaming smile and despite your mood you couldn't help but smile back. Sean has the very rare skill of being empathetic and compassionate; he is an emotional child in the sense that he loves everyone and everything; with Sean the glass is never half empty or half full, it is simply overflowing.

Sean has soon won over the nurses and the doctors with his innocent and random replies to their questions. I once saw him win over the most serious of radiologists without even knowing what he had done. The busy radiographer called Sean, checking his name and address and asking him "Do you know when your birthday is?" Sean looked at the man in utter bewilderment before replying "Yes" in an 'obviously' sort of way. The man, in a rush to complete the scan paused, waiting for confirmation of the date, to which Sean eventually replied "Six sleeps after Christmas!" The radiographer chuckled, smiled and seemed for a moment to forget the arduous day before him. That is Sean's true gift.

His everyday response to the most unfortunate of situations is what makes him so endearing. Driving home one afternoon, our car spun having hit some oil on a wet road. Sean and I were the only ones in the car which spun three times, causing Sean's glasses to come off his face and land in the boot, under the parcel shelf. The first thing he said to me after I eventually got him out of the battered car was "Mummy, I really think you should put the car back on the road."

Unfortunately, that car never saw the road again! Having replaced it a few days later Sean enquired "Is this one a normal car?" Failing to understand what he was meaning and concentrating on my driving, I was lost for a moment and asked what he meant. "It isn't one that goes round and round and round…is it?"

As the doctors change shift Darron returns and I leave Sean, reluctant to go but eager to find out how Mark is. It had been very early that day when I had left him on the doorstep looking forlorn; it now felt like years ago and I was missing

16

him. Of my two sons Mark is much more like me, quieter and thoughtful he contemplates everything and has a habit of overcomplicating things. Mark mostly keeps his emotions and worries to himself and I want to make sure he is alright.

Arriving at my parents' house, they immediately give me a hug and offer me a cup of tea. We have kept them informed all day and there is no more news to tell them and so we talk about Mark, as my mum offers to keep him with them overnight. Mark looks at me and I see the worry in his face as I ask if he wants to stay. He merely shakes his head. I understand completely; under normal circumstances a sleepover at Grandma and Grandad's house is an exciting event, but Mark just wants to go home.

Pulling up outside our home we trudge down the garden path into the house arm in arm. I unlock the door and hear the scamper of our dog's paws on the wooden floor as he eagerly greets us. I put the heating on and make Mark a drink asking if he is hungry, but he has already eaten and I'm not hungry anyway.

It is well past Mark's bedtime and I head upstairs to draw the curtains and sort out the bedroom. The floor is littered with the packaging from the syringes, drugs and paraphernalia; the bed needs stripping and washing, and the phone needs putting back on the cradle. Despite the lateness of the hour I am glad to do something useful. I tuck Mark in and kiss him goodnight and we both know we will be sleeping alone tonight, if sleeping is what you call it.

Following a restless night, I telephone the ward bright and early, knowing that there will be someone on duty to take my call. The ward sister answers and informs me that Sean is fine and will be going home once his medication is arranged. She pauses momentarily before she tells me that he had a bad nosebleed earlier on that morning and a doctor will see us on his ward round. I smile to myself, Sean has been having nosebleeds since he was tiny; quite often I would check on him in bed only to find the sheets red with blood.

I had mentioned this to the social worker and doctors who had been surrounding us at that time in our lives only to be told to keep the information to myself. Apparently nosebleeds can be a sign of child abuse they claimed. I wonder to if they would make that suggestion to the nurses on a hospital ward.

I set off for the hospital much happier than twenty-four hours before, with Mark keen to check on his brother's progress for himself. The discharge takes an age as we are instructed how to administer the emergency rescue medication in case he has another prolonged seizure. I feel better knowing that we have something at home to help in an emergency and we all agree that from where we live getting to any hospital isn't easy.

We pack Sean's bag and Darron carries out a mental check of what we brought with us, Darron had remembered Sean's glasses and some shoes for him to go home in and I am grateful to him. My memory for the everyday things is terrible; I can remember conversations and events from years previously, but never ask me to pick up the milk!

I am handed a number of referral letters for Sean. The cardiologist wants to see him following the discovery of an irregular heartbeat, which I assume might be linked to the hole in the heart he had as a baby. I am also told that Sean will be referred to a haematologist as they are not happy about the bleeding history he has shown and as the questions about his nosebleeds have raised the possibility of a bleeding disorder.

Darron and I both thank the staff and I clutch the referral letters and additional appointments as Darron heaves the bag on to his shoulder and as we walk out the hospital and breathe fresh air it is a relief. Sean skips and twirls happily in front of us, unaware of the situation he has been in and Mark stays reservedly close to me. He is a little nervous of his brother's return home and apprehensive of what the night will bring, but within days the house has returned to normal. In the intervening years since Sean was discharged from the hospital as a baby we have begun to piece our lives back together.

CHAPTER 3.

Both Mark and Sean love school and have a busier social life than either Darron or myself. Sean had shown slight odd movements and vacant stares, but they had been brief and nothing like the extensive brain damage we were led to believe he had suffered. He had met all his milestones ahead of schedule and the only thing he had seemed to struggle with was drawing and writing made worse by the fact he needed glasses. I worried how he would manage but the sudden and dramatic improvement in his sight kept them firmly on his face.

Sean had recently learned to ride a two wheeled bike and spent any fine day whizzing up and down the patio racing Mark. They climbed trees, kicked footballs and ate more than their fair share. Life had been normal again up until that day in February 2009.

The following year went in a round of appointments and hospital visits. Darron had been made redundant and his employer had failed to pay his last months wages and his redundancy pay. I was still only working part time and money was tight. The legal system was difficult to navigate and we had no money to pay a solicitor. In the end we took his employer to court ourselves, serving final demands and paying court fees upfront in order to bring him to a tribunal. The judge awarded all the money without reservation and demanded an additional payment for breach of contract, but we celebrated prematurely as the money never materialised.

Darron had long since gone self-employed, with the recession leading to a massive shortage of jobs, and we were making ends meet - just. It was a tough time and we felt that there was no help for people like us who were trying to work hard and raise a family and do it all above board. There were times when the stress mounted, but we knew we had been in worse situations.

Around this time we had started to take increasing notice of Sean's behaviour, on one occasion I had woken Sean up in the morning and he had been barely conscious. His face looked lopsided and he was refusing to speak. I virtually shouted at him, trying to work out why he wasn't answering before carrying him downstairs to ask Darron's opinion. He seemed able to walk but unable to talk to me and his eyes seemed as if they were trying to communicate desperately. I started to panic only to find that shortly after he spoke and told us he was fine. He couldn't explain why he hadn't been able to talk and ate his breakfast as normal.

Darron took him to the GP, who considered the possibility that it might be a problem with his teeth as the lopsidedness was now gone. Looking back, he probably never needed that emergency dental appointment—they found a small hole in one tooth and filled it anyway—but with hindsight it was a seizure, or the aftermath of one.

We had reported everything to Sean's paediatrician and we felt confident in his care. He had expressed the opinion that the seizure could be a one off episode, but he carried out EEG's and more scans to be safe. Meanwhile, the haematologist had started checking for blood disorders but the results were inconsistent. In fact, every time Sean's blood was tested it would show up different irregularities and we would see different haematologists with different specialities.

Whilst having a day out in August 2010, Sean suddenly stopped dead. My parents had come with us to Sherwood Forest for the day and, as we all exchanged knowing looks, I asked them to continue with Mark. Darron watched as I knelt beside Sean asking him what was wrong and Sean replied "I feel funny". I carried him to a quiet spot, fully anticipating a full seizure, but he merely leaned against me and stopped talking After a few minutes he queried how long we had been there, "Has it been minutes or hours?" He had lost track of time.

Sean got up declaring that he felt better and continued to run around playing chase with his brother. I phoned the hospital when we got home and they made a new appointment to see Sean and discuss what had happened as we were starting to see an increase in the regularity of the seizures and absences. By his seventh birthday in December 2010 we had noticed that the episodes were more frequent when he was tired and we had tried to ensure that he went to bed on time. However, we took him to see a film for his birthday that finished late, sure that a one off late night wouldn't make any difference; the three partial seizures the following day told us otherwise.

Only weeks later, on the 16th January 2011, Sean woke up in the early hours of the morning and I find him retching at the bathroom sink. I ask him what's wrong and he tells me the sickness has passed and he feels fine. As he walks to go past me and into his bedroom there is something about the situation that makes me nervous. I break the rule of a lifetime and ask him to lie down in my bed, Darron enquiring if everything is alright. I am not really sure what's wrong but I sense something is going to happen, that something isn't right.

Sean gradually grows increasingly quiet and as I watch him in the half light of the bedside lamp he is still responding to me but talking in monosyllables. I take the decision to go downstairs and phone the ward that Sean has open access to, getting through to the doctor in a couple of rings. I start to explain the peculiarity of the situation, when Darron's voice bellows from the top step.

"Put the phone down and call an ambulance!" His voice is insistent, the panic obvious and palpable as he repeats

---

the request, swearing so loudly that it causes me to apologise to the doctor on the line as I hang up. I know what has happened as I phone for an ambulance and Darron continues the call as I administer the diazepam we have been given for just such a situation.

As my little boy's body convulses, the king-size bed makes him appear smaller still. I had not put the main light on for fear of hurting his unaccustomed eyes, but soon realise it will be needed when the paramedics arrive. Sean's face has drooped again and his right eye is turned down as his eye lids flutter and he foams at the mouth. His arms are rotating in a strange circular motion and his little legs twitch as I wait for the medication to work.

I am trying to have an unspoken argument with myself in my head, trying to work out how long it has been and if I should wait or administer a second dose, when I hear the paramedics come up the stairs. I am again thankful for the support and I step back to allow them to do their job.

The ambulance crew give more diazepam intravenously and, as the seizure stops they allow us time to pack some things and get dressed before we repeat the ambulance trip we had made nearly a year earlier. As we arrive at the hospital the paramedics take Sean straight to the ward. The seizure has stopped and Sean is stable as they wheel him in silence towards a bed. I notice a father and son trying to sleep in beds opposite, disturbed by our arrival and that of a number of health professionals. Feeling a little guilty for their loss of sleep, I take my place next to Sean's bed, waiting for the round of tests and discussions that will inevitably follow.

I again give a full description of the events of that morning, surprised to learn that the paediatrician on duty is none other than Dr. Fearn, a doctor who had treated Sean so regularly in his infancy and who had played a major role in Sean's life. Darron arrives in time to see the doctor walk on to the ward and, unsure as to whether we would remember him, he smiles and starts to introduce himself again. There is no need. This man had done more for Sean than I could possibly say; he had discharged him home and he had fought the system to help us, he could never be forgotten, he was an unsung hero, who goes to work each day for the benefit of his patients and gives his all.

We greet him as an old friend, shaking hands and filling him in on Sean's progress. Sean, for his part, is recovering his ability to speak and is therefore asking for breakfast. As we chat about what the seizures mean for Sean we all know that things could be worse. Sean is epileptic, but he is not severely brain damaged, he is not confined to a wheelchair and he is not in care.

Before Dr. Fearn discharges Sean we ask our son if he would give one of his special 'loves' to a man to whom he owed so much but could not remember. He obliges eagerly, tottering out of bed, albeit a little unsteadily, and wrapping his arms around the neck of the doctor who kneels before him, squeezing him tight. The poignancy of the moment is not lost on any of us.

It was a few months later, when the many visits to Manchester Children's Hospital with Sean and the many blood tests he'd been having were the last thing on my mind, that the answer to our seven-year battle ended as abruptly as it had started.

Getting ready for work, Mark brought the post from the door, fighting past our West Highland Terrier who was running around him in circles. He flicked through the envelopes declaring that most of them were junk mail before handing an envelope to me directly.

The postal filter service was something Mark often did and I wasn't ever sure why, he always liked to know what was going on and he could tell which letters were hospital ones from the clear franking mark on the front. "This one's for Sean, it's from the hospital." Mark stated with certainty on handing me the letter.

I am busy making the school packed lunches and would normally leave the post until after I get home from work, but since I know the letter is there, it intrigues me. I open the envelope and, before I can read the correspondence, a Special Medical Warning Card flitters out. I turn it over with my heart pounding as I read 'Haemorrhagic States' in big letters and the contact details of the haemophilia centre at the hospital. I abandon the sandwiches and take the card and letter with me as I climb the stairs calling Darron urgently. "I don't believe it", I tell him as he emerges from the bathroom, "They've sent us this, nothing else, just this!"

He reads the letter that is not at all informative and exceptionally brief; it merely asks Sean to carry the warning card with him wherever he goes and to advise any doctor or dentist of the fact that he has 'Storage Pool Disorder'. Darron and I walk downstairs together, chuntering at the lack of further information and declaring after all we've been through we deserve more.

Darron re-sorts the sifted mail and discovers a further letter, addressed to the pair of us, sat at the bottom of the pile; clearly having missed Mark's filtering system. The letter is a copy of the one sent to our GP, confirming Sean's diagnosis but it speaks in medical jargon that we don't understand. I immediately resolve to do the thing doctors hate most and 'Google' it when I get a minute. We had been told by the haematologists that a blood disorder would provide an explanation for the subdural haematoma Sean suffered as a baby and now, as I stand in my kitchen, after everything we have been through, after the legal battle of a lifetime, the news feels hollow.

CHAPTER 4.

Sean Toomey was born on the 31st December 2003 – New Years Eve. His birth in some ways marked the end of a very difficult time for me and the start of a new, even more difficult, one. My husband Darron and I had married in August 1999. We had hoped to get married in the year 2000, for no other reason than we thought I would be able to get a job after recently graduating in Electrical and Electronic Engineering and we would be able to save some money.

Any wedding has the propensity to cost a small fortune, they run away with you. It all seems to be going swimmingly and then you add it up, with table decorations, invites—even the licence—It all has a habit of totting up. To get married in the millennium we discovered was going to cost more than a small private island! So, broke but happy, we planned the wedding for two months after my graduation and one month after my 21st birthday.

Having accidentally double booked us twice, our local priest had actually done us a huge favour, the sun shone on our wedding day and it was hot! For some in August this would be taken for granted, but we live in the Derbyshire hills and sun is something not seen very often. It is certainly almost never accompanied by any sort of heat. A mere hint of blue sky and the supermarkets have run out of burgers and sun cream and everyone is eagerly awaiting a break in cloud to light the barbeque. On that day in August, as we danced the night away as newlyweds, the weather wouldn't have mattered; we were imagining all the great things to come.

Having settled into married life and having already coped with redundancy and stressful house moves, we finally

decided the time was right for a family and shortly after, I discovered I was pregnant. I say discovered, in fact the
sickness gave it away. I confided in a friend at work that I suspected I might be pregnant after being seen frequenting the toilet. The sickness was constant. Once we had a more reliable result by using a traditional pregnancy test rather than a sick-ometer, we looked at each other and silly grins spread across our faces.

We were both thrilled and invited both sets of Grandparents-to-be for a meal with the sole intention of surprising them with the news. It worked. As my mum smothered me in hugs and kisses, my dad sat looking suitably shell-shocked. Darron's dad immediately ordered me a non-alcoholic cocktail complete with cherries and umbrellas! Life it seemed, couldn't get any better.

It was at work the following week that I realised the pregnancy was going to be tough. I was being sick up to five times a day and then the bleeding started. I called the hospital and they arranged for a scan at our local hospital. The sonographer couldn't find anything on the normal scan and prepared us for the possibility that the baby had died. An internal scan was booked just to be sure and there it was, a tiny blip pulsating away. Our baby was alive, but we had a long way to go - I was only nine weeks pregnant.

The bleeding /scan routine became a constant all through my first pregnancy with the start of contractions at twenty-one weeks. Darron was constantly being called at work to tell him I had been taken, yet again, to hospital. I felt incredibly guilty as the ambulance crews constantly had to attend this sick mother who always seemed to be having a crisis.

By the end of the pregnancy my blood pressure had soared and I had pre-eclampsia. I had also started itching everywhere and couldn't sleep. Every night I would sit awake scratching the soles of my feet and the palms of my hands, begging for the pregnancy to be over.

I got my wish when, after another regular daily blood pressure check, the midwife confirmed I was in labour, two weeks early but not a moment too soon. After twelve hours I I went to our local birthing centre, but my blood pressure was sky-rocketing and, taking no chances, they sent me off to the bigger hospital by ambulance - again.

A further day passed with me in labour and with midwives occasionally bobbing in. Darron's eyes were showing a glazed look as we spent the night in the delivery suite and still no baby had arrived. The midwives checked progress and told me that I was 'stuck' at four centimetres dilated. The senior midwife dutifully advised me that "It could be another several hours yet".

Several hours? Who were they kidding? There was no way I could take several more hours, having only had gas and air I decided that, contrary to my birth plan, I would agree to more pain relief. (For those of you who don't already know, a birth plan is a document that you draw up with your midwife. She smiles and nods encouragingly when you mention things like 'water-birth', 'natural' and 'minimal intervention'. I have never yet met a woman whose baby followed the birth plan, they are blissfully ignorant of the document even if you read it aloud.)

Darron was about to go and get a breakfast snack, following the news that he would have to forgo a fry-up in place of sitting awaiting his first-born, when they gave me some Pethidine. Within seconds though, now feeling more dizzy than anything else I declared I needed to push. The midwife waved me away with a hand saying "Have a little push if you like but we checked and you have ages yet". The dismissive and almost delighted way she said this made me wonder if she had ever had children. I found out later that she was newly expecting her first (I hope she had her birth plan ready). I then declared that if it wasn't the baby, I needed the toilet.

What happened next is really quite surreal and if there hadn't been witnesses I would swear that it was in fact the Pethidine. I went into the toilet, Darron told by the midwife to trundle the gas and air and the midwife and a colleague all following. Not sure why my bodily functions were of such great entertainment to all present, I looked a little affronted. I am normally a very reserved person, the sort who pins her towel to her chest with her chin and gets dressed behind it at the swimming baths. I wasn't keen on the audience.

Things became even more unhinged when the midwife's hand shot between my legs. "That's the head!" She declares in a shocked voice, "Walk back to the bed." Pethidine or not, I'm not that out of it as I exclaim, "You want me to *walk*?" So all of us, like a very badly put together pantomime horse, manage to get back to the bed and moments later Mark is born.

Having been kneeling up on the bed, Mark was passed to me for that very precious first cuddle. I can honestly say that all I remember thinking was 'he's blue!' before the Pethidine really took hold and the room swam. Mark was rescued from me as I lost my bearings and passed out.

On the plus side I recommend Pethidine for anyone having stitches. I barely remember a thing. Darron was given the honour of the first cuddles and through my haze, all I can remember is him saying to me "He's perfect, can we have another?"

Even after transferring back to our local cottage hospital, the midwives were amazed at how loud Mark was when he cried. Upon returning home he fed hourly but then projectile vomited straight over everything in range and, trust me, it was some range! I kept being told that I was a new mum and 'that's what babies do', yet other mums expressed how sorry they felt for me, he was *that* loud. In the end I pushed him in his pram, screaming like a siren to the local health visitor, Karen. She took one look at him and we were at the Children's Hospital that afternoon.

Even at the hospital the nursing staff were a little dismissive. We had planned the pregnancy and had been married a couple of years but at twenty-three I was still a relatively young mum. I got the distinct impression that they didn't trust my judgement. By nightfall we were told there was nowhere for us to stay with him, he was on a mixed age ward and the only place we could go to was to the 'parent house' some distance away. The parent rooms were all full, some with several members of the same family staying.

Half pushed by the nurses and dragged by my husband I reluctantly went home and spent the remainder of the night packing stuff for Mark, crying and clock watching. At the crack of dawn we drove the hour and a half back to the hospital at my insistence, it wasn't even 6.00a.m. When we got to the ward it was still early and the curtains were still closed. We didn't need to open the door though to recognise the screaming of our baby son.

Upon entering we were greeted by the sight of a nurse frantically rocking Mark in a sprung Silver Cross pram, bouncing the wheels and pushing him back and forth. The nurse ventured needlessly "He's not stopped crying all night, he's kept the whole ward awake!" I thought to myself; we told *you* that.

It turned out Mark had a problem with his bowels, food was not passing through and had therefore started to come back up. He was crying as he was so hungry and the constant screaming hadn't helped the umbilical hernia he had developed. The consultants ran around him, carrying out tests and then procedures. When he eventually came home with his large pack of medication the silence was deafening.

CHAPTER 5.

Before we had even started our family we had set our hearts on two 'munchkins'. We had hoped that we would have a playmate for Mark and we had also planned that, if possible, they would be close in age. Having sold our first marital home only days after Mark's birth, we finally moved out days before his Christening in July 2002. I was thrilled to find out I was pregnant in November and we delightedly started telling people around Christmas time. It was Mark's first Christmas and although he had no idea what it was all about he loved the lights and the baubles.

Visitors to our house were greeted by a rather unusual sight. Mark at nine months could already pull himself to stand and cruise – he was only ten months old when he walked. So by far the safest thing we thought so as to let him have his new found freedom, was instead of putting Mark in the playpen, to put the Christmas tree in! So the six-foot tree, decorated with shining glass baubles, shimmering tinsel and twinkling lights was surrounded by a matt-white metal playpen. Not really the look I was going for but practical all the same!

The day after Boxing Day I started bleeding and we drove in silence back to the hospital we had travelled to so many times before, with Mark in the back babbling away. Once there they informed me I was miscarrying. I was bleeding very heavily but they told me the wards were full. The doctor gave me a prescription for painkillers and advised me to see my GP.

We drove home in silence that day too. I rang work and informed them of what had happened but I was greeted with the message that they were short staffed. In a blur I arrived at work the following day but collapsed at lunchtime. New Year was a complete washout.

It wasn't long after I had recovered when all I could think about was being pregnant again. We didn't bother with contraception as we were barely functioning let alone anything else. One night we started to talk about what had happened and we consoled each other with the fact we could try again. Within a fortnight we had decided that perhaps it was too soon and I made arrangements to see the GP about a prescription for the pill.

Clearly it wasn't too soon because within days I felt the familiar sickness I had felt on the previous two occasions. I was pregnant for the third time and we were quietly rejoicing. I spoke to the doctor, not sure if there was an increased chance of miscarrying so soon after our previous loss. He informed me that there was no evidence that this was the case and that I just needed to rest and take it easy, adding his congratulations as he hung up the phone.

We decided that after the stress of having to inform people that I was no longer pregnant we wouldn't tell anyone this time until things were a little further along. As per both my previous pregnancies I started to bleed and with no A&E department in any direction within half an hour, we set off for what seemed a very prolonged drive in silence. The nurses at the hospital were lovely and, as with Mark, the scan showed nothing. They ordered an internal one to check but they needn't have bothered as I started bleeding heavily on the table. I walked back to the nurses' office but barely made it; I was doubled up. I was gently told that I was in the process of miscarrying and they then asked for a urine sample in a jug to check the hormone levels. Everything came away in the jug.

I didn't know what to do and was panic stricken. I felt like I couldn't flush the contents away, but I couldn't look either. On top of all that I had to walk up the ward back to the nurse's office, past rows of mums cradling babies. I covered the jug with paper towels, left it on the nurse's desk and ran out crying hysterically.

Darron followed me, unsure of what had happened, and the nurse found me shortly after. I will never forget the kindness shown to me that day by the staff at that hospital. The nurses allowed me to stay in their office until I had composed myself and their calm and reassuring manner meant everything.

People often say that you shouldn't tell people in the early stages of pregnancy in case something happens. I don't really think it matters either way. The first time I miscarried I had the terrible job of telling people what had happened but also the opportunity to share the shock and grief with them. Family and friends had been excited on our behalf and were just as crushed to learn that things had gone wrong.

The second time we were left with just the two people we had confided in; my mum and my dad. This was mainly because we needed someone to help us with Mark while we were at the hospital. I was left feeling as if it hadn't happened. My body still felt pregnant and everybody thought I should have been recovering from the first miscarriage by that time when I had suffered a second. It seemed pointless to say 'I was pregnant, but I'm not now' so I just kept quiet.

For those people who want to know what to say to someone who's lost a baby don't say any of the following:

1) 'It was for the best' – Why? Do you know something I don't?
2) 'It was probably disabled' – It a) wouldn't have mattered and b) refer to 1.
3) 'At least you won't have to endure the birth' – I'm not even going to answer that one.

Stick to things like "I'm very sorry" or "If you need anything" and remember that men grieve too. Dads have also lost a baby and they have shared in the expectation of becoming a Father.

Lots of people directing fathers to help, like some sort of traffic marshal, really doesn't provide support. Time really only heals well after everyone else has already forgotten and moved on.

Bearing in mind the medical profession will have a huge part in what would happen to our family, following the second miscarriage I visited a GP' who worked at the doctor's surgery, for a completely unrelated reason. The doctor immediately launched into an attack about my waste of NHS resources, which left me hurt and confused. I had to interject to ask him what he was referring to. He looked straight at me and said "You missed your ante-natal appointment."

I replied "But I'm not pregnant."

He continued in a vehement tone; "You are, I have the results here and an appointment was made that *you* missed". I couldn't believe what I was listening to. Macclesfield Hospital's headed notepaper was sticking out of the top of my medical notes. The only time I had been there was following the miscarriage. My voice was quivering as I added apologetically; "I miscarried, the notes will be in that letter I think", pointing to the notepaper that was visibly at the front of my notes. I came home furious. How dare a doctor tell me off for wasting resources, when he hadn't read the notes!

By the time I became pregnant for the fourth time I never bothered with a pregnancy test. The sickness started in earnest and within a short space of time the itching that was to plague me from then on started too. We made the decision to tell close family only and that was proven to be the right thing to do when I started to bleed again.

This time, I went back to Stockport's new early pregnancy unit and the staff were brilliant. They had obviously listened to the views of women who don't want to be on wards with babies, when they have lost theirs and thought more about women who don't want to be surrounded by mums cradling bumps, when they think they are losing theirs. On this occasion the medical profession and the hospital had got it right.

The scan on the main screen showed nothing and again they wanted to do an internal one. I refused. Last time following the scan I had bled severely. That picture still haunted me and I didn't want to go there again. Darron, desperate for answers, implored me without saying a word. The nurse cajoled me, making a promise to give me an illicit print-off of the picture if the baby was still living. I relented. The sonographer operated the scanner in silence as I, trying not to get my hopes up, waited for her professional opinion. It didn't take years of training to see what was on that screen, a small shape not unlike a kidney bean showed on the monitor and in part of it pulsed a heartbeat.

I clutched the scan picture for all it was worth as the sonographer smiled, happy to share in our joy. It wasn't the sort of scan picture you could show people, it wasn't really recognisable as such, but to Darron and me it was hope and we named it our 'beanie-baby'. The pregnancy progressed with the same bumpy ride I had experienced the first time. I suffered from bleeding throughout the early stages of the pregnancy and what the doctor referred to as a 'missed-miscarriage', but our 'beanie-baby' clung on. I realised that pregnancy and me were not at all compatible.

I went to work part-time, taught music in the evenings after Mark had gone to bed, and ran around after him when he got up. I didn't drive, so everywhere I went I had to walk. That didn't really faze me though; it kept me, Mark and the dog fit. It did, however, make the frequent appointments difficult. Thankfully my Grandma, who lived in the same village, was always on hand in an emergency. I could bless her little Peugeot!

Throughout the pregnancy, whilst the bleeding kept occurring, the itching increased. With Mark, they had told me that I had developed Obstetric Cholestasis, a condition in which there is a problem with bile flow in the liver causing bile to enter the bloodstream. Bile salts cause itching, which started in my hands and feet and eventually spread. The itch is persistent, worse at night and kept me awake for hours. In order to get some sleep, I would fill a bowl with the coldest water I could run from the tap and add ice, if I could, in order to freeze my feet and hands numb. If I was quick and got straight in to bed I found I could get two hours sleep until it started again.

By the end of my pregnancy nothing worked. I couldn't sleep. I had developed pre-eclampsia again and, possibly due to having the window open in December to keep cool from itching, I had developed a hacking cough that left me crawling round the floor on all fours trying to catch my breath.

By the time I saw the obstetrician again I was really down. He had already advised me that there was an increased risk of stillbirth and that we would probably have to deliver the baby early. Due to the miscarriages I didn't really know when the baby was due exactly – the earliest date was the first week in February but scans showed the baby was possibly due before. Unless my biology was really off whack, I could tell them that February was definitely the earliest date.

I was still dragging myself to work and had decided that, unlike with Mark where I had taken maternity leave only days before he arrived, I would be sensible. I booked my leave from Christmas Eve giving me a good month to prepare. By the week before Christmas 2003 they had decided that the induction would have to be soon. I was getting worse, my urine was now orange and I hadn't slept in months.

I finished work on Christmas Eve and despite everything I was in good spirits. Christmas is always a great time in our house. Darron and I are both Christmas crazy and the house is decked all over. I was looking forward to seeing

---

37

Mark open his presents, looking forward to the new arrival and I had finished work for a while, meaning that I could put my feet up in the final weeks of my pregnancy.

Christmas was all I could have wished for, except for the itching that drove me to the verge of insanity. We had stayed with my parents over Christmas as we usually did because I didn't drive it meant Darron could have a drink. Mum went to town on the food (she is a great cook) and Dad kept the drinks flowing (Vimto for me).

I still couldn't sleep and was itching all over, with my face the newest body part to be added to the list. For the past few months the bruising, which was always a problem for me, had reached new heights. My thighs were covered in bruises the size of an adult shoe. Darron was with me when I saw the obstetrician on the morning of the thirtieth of December for an outpatient's appointment and was immediately admitted.

My relationship with hospitals has been a long one. Since being born prematurely myself I have had frequent trips, with a variety of long term conditions. In fact, as we speak, I have four appointments booked with three different departments! As my mum always said, with me she didn't get the plans right. Therefore I have grown to hate everything about hospitals, the dry air, the waiting and the lack of any sort of action until things reach ridiculous proportions. I had, therefore, been admitted to hospital three times previously but signed myself out. There was nothing they could offer me in my own private torture other than 'monitoring'. At home I could leave the windows open whilst it snowed and take a deep breath before plunging my extremities into ice. I could watch TV with a fan on full and, in short, could try to make life a little bit easier for myself.

On this particular day my obstetrician was on leave and I had been sent to the ward for yet more blood tests awaiting the arrival of the obstetrician on duty. A midwife scolded me saying, "You shouldn't be on the ward in bare feet—you need slippers!" As I hurriedly explained I had come up from outpatients. She nodded, countering that she would have to fill in the paperwork, whilst she assigned me a bed. Darron went home to get some things for me, not least of all my slippers.

It wasn't long afterwards that my own obstetrician came walking up the ward with several students in tow. After the initial greetings I asked him why he wasn't on holiday and he replied that as one of his 'complicated ladies' had been admitted he had been called to attend, looking straight at me as he spoke. He flicked through the latest results in my notes as I smiled, knowing, by his manner, that he was referring to me. At the word 'admission' he must have seen the defiant look in my eyes and because we had come to know each other quite well of late he quickly added, "You needn't think about leaving. The next time you go home it will be with that baby, we're inducing you today."

I should possibly have felt panicked, particularly when he explained that I wouldn't be allowed pain relief other than gas and air, in case of an emergency caesarean section. He explained that if things went really haywire he couldn't promise a nice bikini line cut either and he made me sign the permission form then and there.

I didn't feel panic. I had already been through one labour and had I known that the baby was so near being born I would not have agreed to the Pethidine anyway. If things did go so wrong there would be nothing I could do about it, lots of women have caesarean sections and, although I know it isn't an easy option, after feeling so ill for so long the idea of finally having my baby and being free of the itching made anything seem worthwhile. I made a quick call to Darron and then I made my way, accompanied by two nurses, to delivery.

The induction went ahead, as they warned me that it was a last ditch attempt. I was given everything they had and for my part I kept 'mobilising'. This may seem more like something an army might have done but apparently moving around a lot helps the labour. Boy did I move around a lot! I stayed still only for them to monitor the baby's heart rate and then kept pacing.

The first midwife went off shift, the second midwife went off shift and things were not progressing. I was stuck at four centimetres dilated (no surprise there!) I was tired. I had only come in for an ante-natal appointment and, by this point, I had been up for over twenty four hours straight with barely any sleep in months.

I remember lying on the bed briefly and the midwife half encouraging, half pulling me up after fifteen minutes rest in order to keep the contractions strong. That was the only time in the fifteen and a half hour labour that I lay on the bed at all. I had 'mobilised' to within an inch of my life, but if it prevented a caesarean section, then mobilise I would.

When the second midwife went off shift I was greeted by a very jovial Jamaican midwife who was buxom and motherly. She was great, just the right sort of person you need to keep your spirits up and stern enough to keep you mobilised! She had also brought with her a student midwife, who was hoping to deliver the baby. I was surprised that after such intense monitoring and close observation by the obstetricians, that a student was going to deliver the baby but, in the absence of the stork, quite frankly by this point the postman could have delivered it!

At around 9.00a.m. I moved into a position, leaning on the bed that felt almost comfortable. I heard Darron tell the midwives, "I hope whoever is planning to deliver this baby has their catch mitt on. They both laughed as he added, "I'm serious, she did this last time and our eldest nearly ended up in the toilet."

Everything seemed to take place very quickly but to me I was too busy concentrating on me and my body to care about any of it. They got me on to the bed and as they ran around getting on gloves the more senior midwife shouted "Don't push, don't push!" Who are they kidding? Nothing on earth could stop me after all that. My body was acting on instinct and I had no energy or inclination to fight it. The gloves were barely on when the student midwife was steered in to position just in time to deliver our newest arrival: Sean, on New Year's Eve 2003.

CHAPTER 6.

I had often wondered, having already had a baby boy, if Darron wanted a little girl. After everything I had been through I was content with a living, breathing baby of either sex. Part of me thought that, although he had always said he didn't mind, he might be disappointed with another little boy.

There was nothing he had ever done that had made me think it, it is just that in his family there were all boys. His mum had longed for a daughter but given birth to sons, and now she longed for a granddaughter following two grandsons. The wondering ended there and then though as I heard the midwife say to him, "Tell her what she's had." Darron turned to me with tears in his eyes and announced: "A little boy, it's a little boy. No pink aisle for us! It'll be Scalectrix next Christmas!" I think we would have both been pleased either way, but I can put my hand on my heart and say that I have loved every minute of having sons.

The part immediately following delivery got quite busy. Once I had showered and applied a bit of make-up for the post delivery photo shoot I re-joined Darron and Sean. Darron had complained that after the birth of Mark the photos I had taken of him were blurred or headless and I defended myself by informing him that post-delivery most mums are not up to playing David Bailey!

The midwife had started to look very busy looking at charts, doing a heel-prick test for glucose as I noticed, like Mark, Sean was blue, but unlike Mark he was also cold. The midwife took another look at him and stated that he was more premature than they'd first thought, possibly thirty-five weeks. She handed him to me stating that I should keep him wrapped up and cuddle him close to keep him warm.

I asked if he was alright as she was looking worried and she replied that she thought he would normally go into an incubator adding "We'll see. You want him home don't you?" We would later find out that at this point he was suffering from hypothermia. After the initial rush, things calmed down and they put Sean in one of those little see-though cribs with some sort of monitor on him. To this day, I have no idea what it was and neither does my husband, we were just happy to be a mum and dad all over again. The midwives didn't seem too concerned and we trusted their judgement.

As Darron went to add another parking ticket on the car, I lay on the bed for what I considered a well-deserved rest. I felt elated. We had always wanted two children and here they were safe and well. I was overjoyed, tired but thrilled. 'How clever am I?' I thought to myself and 'definitely no more pregnancies!'

I hadn't been laid down for long when I heard a commotion outside the door. I couldn't make out much of what was being said other than 'test results', 'dangerous levels', and 'immediate delivery'. Upon hearing the last part I remember thinking, 'oh dear, another woman having a rough time.' I had just started to drift when the same voice added, "Toomey." My eyes darted to the door when in burst a man in a green theatre gown, his mask around his neck. He started to talk very fast and, whilst doing so, he took the brakes off the wheels on the bed and started to roll it away from the wall.

Tired and confused I tried to concentrate on what he was saying when I grasped that they needed to deliver the baby urgently as the latest blood test results, the ones they had taken the day before, showed a serious problem. Stuttering, and unable to speak from the shock of the intrusion, I pointed over to the crib waving at it in panic.

Steadily the doctor pushed the bed back to the wall and walked over to where Sean lay. Looking into the cot he looked back at me and a smile spread across his face. He looked back at Sean and exclaimed, "You made it little guy! Amazing, you made it! Happy Birthday." With that he nodded to me and walked out of the room. To this day I don't know who he was or why he wasn't told I'd had the baby. What I did know was the last thing I needed was a caesarean section after all. Darron retuned from the car park and I filled him in on the surprise visit and, as I did so, the midwife came in to ask me why I had refused vitamin K for Sean. I had stated that I was happy for him to have whatever was felt necessary. I was taking vitamin K supplements prescribed due to the liver problems and bruising I was having and she asked if I had taken them that day. I stated that since I was admitted from an ante-natal appointment my medication was at home.

Nothing more was said other than that I found out a little later that the student had signed to say Sean had been given vitamin K orally. This was unusual as it needs to be repeated and most babies born in Britain are given vitamin K by injection shortly after birth to prevent Vitamin K deficiency bleeding. About half of babies who suffer this bleeding problem die or sustain significant brain-damage due to bleeding into the brain.

The midwife was sure that the confusion had arisen because I was taking oral vitamin K. In fact Sean hadn't had any, but they were unable to give him some until they had checked with the student that she hadn't actually administered it and she had already gone home.

Despite Sean's low body temperature the midwife came back and told us that she thought if we kept cuddling him we could 'get away' with not sending him to special care. Much later we were left wondering if he should have been sent to special care after all, especially as Darron and I realised that before they had contacted the student midwife about the vitamin K, we had been transferred and nothing more was said to us about it. A mistake that could have been fatal.

It was a strange New Year as I settled in to the local cottage hospital on my own. I had missed breakfast whilst delivering Sean and as I was awaiting transfer, I never went up to the ward for lunch either. By the time the transfer was complete and I arrived at the local Hospital I had just missed tea.

As it was New Year's Eve the staff were all bank staff and apparently the people who delivered the lunches had put sandwiches aside for me, but they had been taken for a New Year get together on another ward as I was so late arriving. Tired, hungry and unable to share my big news with everyone as they were all out for New Year, I went to bed and fell asleep at ten minutes to midnight.

Late morning the following day, Darron arrived with Mark, lamenting the fact that all the florists were closed. I confess that I do have a secret love of flowers, so long as they are not on curtains or wallpaper. I pretend not to be bothered either way and often laugh when people present flowers as a token of their undying love – not very undying when less than a week later you are throwing out brownish stems and green water!

I knew the thought was there and nothing could dampen my pride at having managed not one but two gorgeous boys. I took a photo (in focus this time) of Darron holding Mark holding Sean. It is still one of my favourites as Mark, not even two, looks adoringly into his little brother's eyes.

The world seemed calm as we stayed a day or two more at my mum and dad's before finally heading home. Everyone who saw Sean commented on how quiet he was. In the first two weeks my parents saw him, they never saw his eyes open. He seemed to feed half asleep and I woke him rather than the other way around. We had given the hospital my mum and dad's number but nobody had called.

We weren't worried, the danger had passed and Sean had arrived safe and sound. We revelled in our luck getting an easy second baby following Mark's rousing dawn chorus! I was still plagued by itching, but I knew that, in time, that would go along with my bruises.

We arrived home on a Monday. I only remember because I had planned to go to playgroup to meet friends and then remembered that it was still the Christmas holidays. I had taken maternity leave on Christmas Eve to give me time to prepare, but as it happened I hadn't been home since. The house was cold as we walked in and we immediately put the heating on and made a cup of tea. Darron did at least half a dozen trips with all Mark's new Christmas toys, high chair and now Sean's gifts. I looked out at the snow and thought a person can't get any luckier than this.

However, within days things had started to take a rather unsettling turn. Emma, the community midwife, had left a note for us as she hadn't been told by the hospital that I was staying with my parents. I called her straight away and she came first thing the following morning. As Emma read the notes she raised her eyebrows and commented that she was a little surprised at how soon Sean was discharged. I wasn't sure why she felt like this and, with a two year old determined to join in the conversation at every point, it was hard to hold a full conversation. Emma seemed pleased with Sean's progress and she marvelled at how Mark had grown since she had last seen him as a baby.

It was later that night that we first spotted that Sean had a bluish tinge. At first we thought it might be the odd snowy light for the time of year, and as soon as it had appeared it seemed to disappear. He was also making strange jerky movements, which we had been told were normal in small babies. Sean was now also showing obvious signs of jaundice and we were advised to put him in the daylight as much as possible. The yellow colour of his skin made it harder to see any tinge, blue or otherwise.

Sean was only two weeks old and Darron had returned to work when I noticed Sean had a definite blue colour. It was worse around his lips, but his eyes looked almost sunken as if he hadn't slept for a week. He was very lethargic, but was still feeding alright and I wasn't sure what to do next. I resolved to ring the midwife at our local cottage hospital who advised me that this colouring was common in newborns and was due to wind. Having already had one baby, I was unsure but didn't feel able to question the medical opinion I was getting from a professional. That is something that today I wouldn't hesitate to do but at the time I trusted her, perhaps too much.

I rang again in the following days and by the time Darron had finished his last shift at work, I was glad to have someone in the house with me. On Wednesday the twenty-first of January 2004, when Sean was three weeks old, he went blue again and then a waxy white colour. He had taken his last feed at 1.00p.m. in the afternoon and when his next feed was due at around 3.30p.m. we couldn't rouse him.

It was quite normal that he was sleeping a lot but, even so, he never missed a feed completely. By around 5.00p.m. I had decided to give him a bath hoping to wake him up.
As I bathed him in the warm water he stirred slightly but something wasn't right and I couldn't put my finger on what it was. Sean looked completely normal apart from his sleepy demeanour but I was starting to feel agitated and on edge.

I lifted him out of the bath and dried him off but as I did so I realised he wasn't breathing. I placed him on the floor to check but could feel no breaths. I had received plenty of first aid training for adults, knew the ins and outs of CPR, but in terror I screamed repeatedly for Darron, who climbed the stairs in pairs and rushed into the bathroom. As I lifted him up off the floor to pass him to Darron I heard a tiny gasp.

Now my self confidence had deserted me. Had I imagined it? Was he breathing and I had just not felt it? I was sure his breathing had stopped, but, if so, how had it started again? I wondered if I had just panicked too readily.

Darron and I went through the options. If we called an ambulance and he was just sleepy, we would tie up an emergency vehicle without just cause. We knew we couldn't do anything and the local hospital had no A&E. We could drive Sean back to Stockport in forty-five minutes but, if anything happened, we wouldn't be able to take any action as the A6 is a notoriously busy and congested route.

We decided to call NHS Direct and ask them if we should call an ambulance or risk the drive. I placed a call and within a minute the practitioner phoned back. They were reassuring and professional, running through what had happened, but the decision was made for us as Darron yelled from the living room that he thought Sean had stopped breathing again. An ambulance was dispatched immediately and we prayed we hadn't made the worst mistake of our lives by being too cautious.

It seemed to take a lifetime, as we dressed Mark and got him ready for Grandma's house, whilst taking it in turns to gently talk to Sean and move his arms and legs in a ridiculous attempt to keep him breathing. I heard the sirens and within minutes two ambulance crews had converged on the house. Almost immediately, the blue colour that Sean's face had displayed whilst he had appeared to stop breathing had gone again. I was left feeling that maybe we were both somehow losing the plot as the ambulance driver stated that Sean looked merely sleepy rather than ill.

It was decided, as a precaution, to take him to hospital due to his young age and the additional ambulance crew left to attend another call. As I climbed into the ambulance I read a poster about wasting NHS resources and prayed that they wouldn't think that of us. I was less than reassured when the ambulance kept jolting and making terrible noises, only to be told that the ambulance we were travelling in had already been written off for scrap! Within a short space of time all of that became the least of our worries.

CHAPTER 7.

On arrival at the hospital I wait in a curtained cubicle, I presume that we are in the emergency department, but I haven't taken any notice of my surrounds, being shepherded in by the paramedics and now sitting on a plastic chair, cradling my new baby. A paediatrician pulls back the curtain and comes in with at least one other doctor. He asks me to retell the story of Sean's birth and what has happened since. A bed is found up on the children's ward at the hospital and we traipse up there with a heavy heart, trying to second guess what is going to happen next.

The second night, Darron goes home to look after Mark and I try to get some sleep on the small camp bed in Sean's room. The breathing alarms go off several times and nurses rush in and check on him, eventually a doctor decides to carry out a lumbar puncture. A lumbar puncture test is where a large needle is inserted into the spine in order to withdraw spinal fluid for testing. I am told that after the lumbar puncture Sean will have to stay still in order to prevent unwanted side effects.

I agreed to the test but when the time came I couldn't hand over my son. I had worried for him, cared for him and I didn't want to let him out of my sight. No matter how much the nurse encouraged me and told me it was the right thing to do, I couldn't let go of my grip on him. It wasn't a rational thought process, just a fierce protective instinct. Every time the nurse tried to take him from my arms I refused to let go, I just couldn't let go. In the end it is agreed that I can stay with him and despite warnings that it will be distressing to watch, I feel it is the only way I can consent.

The nurse takes us down the corridor to a treatment room where several doctors and more nurses are waiting.

Once there, they curl Sean up like a hedgehog in a tight ball, as I hold his miniature hand, and for the first time in days, he screams as if his lungs will collapse. I try to reassure him with words but they are inaudible over the crying. Then, to my horror, the doctor who had explained the procedure stands to one side and beckons over a student asking him if he would 'like to try the procedure'.

As I look to the nurse and start to object, the student is already inserting the needle into my baby's spine. Three times he inserts it and three times he gets it wrong: as he goes to draw the liquid there is nothing. With both Sean and myself in tears, they eventually abandon the attempt and leave Sean to recover.

The more senior of the two doctors comes back later that night and tries again, unsuccessfully, twice more as blood eventually comes from the site and it is all that is collected from the needle. By now, Sean has been put through hell. Adults are sedated due to the pain lumbar punctures cause, but not tiny babies, who are easy to subdue and, lets face it, if I wasn't there, who would have been any the wiser as to what happened?

In the early hours another unsuccessful attempt means that the ward sister's insistence that a doctor from the special care baby unit carry out the procedure is heeded. The sister comes to apologise to me and tells me that she had advised from the start that, due to Sean's age and size, it would be better asking for a neonatal specialist. The specialist arrives and manages to obtain a sample on the first attempt, but they can't erase what I have seen.

In the early hours of the morning Sean has a seizure and we suddenly realise that there is something more to the lethargy and the breathing problems than his early birth. Tests are booked and the word 'meningitis' is mentioned, as Sean is immediately prescribed phenobarbitone to prevent further fits. The whole world seems to stop on its axis. Surely it must have, for nothing else matters.

My baby, our baby, who had fought so hard to make it into the world, is now struggling to stay. We spend hours staying by his cot, listening to the heart rate monitor bleep and watching as blood tests and other tests are carried out. We are asked if he had fitted previously and reply 'no' but a nurse advises us that fits in babies are not necessarily like fits in adults. We discuss between us the 'jitteriness' that Sean had constantly displayed and the epilepsy in the family.

Whilst we wait for the results of the lumbar puncture a CT scan is requested. We are worried when the scan doesn't happen: we are concerned that the delay may affect Sean's treatment. We were so wrong. It would be the CT scan that would start a ball rolling that, in the end, would take seven years to come to a complete halt.

Sean is fed and wrapped tightly in the hope that he will keep still for the scan. Sean, in his usual fashion, sleeps through it all. As we come back to the ward, Darron and I grab a drink from the parents' room and call my parents to let them know that we are now just waiting for results. There is nothing else to do but sit and keep Sean company. He isn't old enough to play, even if he was well enough, and he isn't aware of his surroundings.

The days and nights are lonely whilst we try to spread our time between our ill baby and our toddler, who when visiting Sean takes much more interest in the playroom. Mark constantly asks "Where Shawny?" but he has spent very little time with him that it is if he never arrived. The stress is immense as we wait for news. When it finally comes though, it doesn't seem to shed any light.

Dr. Fearn, the paediatrician who had been overseeing Sean's care, beckons us out of Sean's room and on to the small corridor, where the light is much brighter. There he tells us he has the CT scan of Sean's brain and holds it to the light for us to see. The black film with the ghostly image means nothing to us, we don't know what it is we are seeing as he points with his pen to parts of Sean's brain that look black. We are told that the black part represents an infarction, meaning permanent damage, and another part which shows a subdural haematoma, a brain haemorrhage in a specific area between the brain and the inside of the skull.

We had always known that meningitis could be potentially fatal but Sean had shown a small, but noticeable, improvement and we are completely unprepared for the news that our son's brain is damaged. Darron and I assume that this is due to the infection Sean is fighting, as Dr. Fearn sits down with us and explains what the damage will mean. Sean may develop Cerebral Palsy; he may have little sight, he may never roll over or sit up; he may never be 'normal'.

In those few minutes every dream we had wished for our son vanished. It no longer mattered if he met his milestones, if he did any of the things that a child his age could do; all that mattered was that he'd kept breathing. Despite all that though, I had one more prayer that I felt guilty asking for: Let him love us, let him show he cares, let him smile. I thought I could cope with anything if my son loved me, if I knew he was happy in life. I didn't know if it was an ask too far.

Sean was now stable, his breathing was fine and there had been no more fits. We were told that the doctors were not clear on what the scan showed. Having spoken to a doctor at Hope Hospital in Salford, Dr. Fearn advised us that Sean would have to be moved to the Children's Hospital in order for him to have an MRI scan and see more specialist doctors.

Dr. Fearn informed us that he had written a letter to the hospital stating that he had no concerns and he told us about the letter in an apologetic tone. We failed to see the significance believing it to be a standard letter, as he merely stated that at the Children's Hospital they had been known to be 'proactive.' He had paused before adding the last word, hesitating and trying to phrase the sentence carefully and professionally before adding, "We know what Pendlebury can be like." We still didn't get the point.

On Tuesday 27th January, we wait all day for Sean's transfer to take place. We feed Sean and change him and still we wait. By 6.00p.m. we decide that we will both go home to see Mark and tuck him in to bed. We are advised that there is no rush to return as there is no way a transfer will take place so late on in the day. Sean is finally looking much better; he has a more pinkish tone, although he is still pale. We both hear the staffs reassurance that we can follow the ambulance to the Children's Hospital in the morning.

The following morning we awake early ready to drive the one and a half hour journey to Pendlebury, Manchester. However, as we look outside we notice a problem. It has snowed heavily and the snow keeps falling. We look up at the sky and all we can see are the clouds, dense with more snowfall. Darron tries in vain to dig out the car, but the faster he digs the car out the faster the snow falls.

In desperation, I call the hospital to tell them we aren't going to make it on time. The ward sister lets me know that Sean had already gone in an ambulance at 7.30p.m. the previous evening, only an hour and a half after we had left. Sean was already there in Manchester and we had no hope of getting to him. I hang up the phone angry. They had promised we would be able to follow him, as the ambulance was full with the specialist incubator needed to transport him and the remaining space was only enough for the accompanying paramedic. It was the start of a period where the medics called the shots and we rolled with the punches.

Although Sean had been too weak to breastfeed from me, I had expressed milk and then bottle fed him. Any mum who has expressed milk will realise that this is not as easy as it seems. If you manage to find a half-decent pump that works, without turning your boobs into something approaching a pointed Madonna basque, and that actually manages to collect milk you're lucky! Now I realised that I couldn't even feed my son, he was miles away, without me. I broke down in floods of tears.

The phone rings mid-morning whilst I am playing with Mark. I try to sound upbeat as we fit shapes into a sorter, put jigsaws together and draw pictures for 'Shawny'. When the ring tone makes me jump I leap up to grab the phone, dreading what the call might be. Everyone we knew, was aware we would be at the hospital, the only people who knew otherwise *were* the hospital.

"Hello? Can I help?" I venture, listening with dread for bad news. The voice on the other end of the line sounds deep and formal, a doctor stating his lengthy title and his place of work as Manchester Children's Hospital. They know there is no way we can make it through the snow and want us to give permission over the phone for an MRI scan. Due to the length of the scan and Sean's age it would be necessary to anaesthetise him. I ask the doctor if he will call back in ten minutes whilst I go to find Darron, who is still vainly trying to release the car from its snow dome.

We stand in the living room knowing we have no choice. We want Sean to get any tests that the doctors feel would be helpful in his treatment. As we discuss the matter with some urgency we both feel angry. Nobody had felt it necessary to tell us our son was being moved, even though we had left only an hour or so earlier. Apparently the Children's Hospital has already scheduled the MRI scan without letting us know. They need our permission but it is a formality; the time slot is booked and the staff are ready.

As the phone rings again we stand side by side and agree first to one doctor and then to another, as they spell out the risk of a general anaesthetic on a tiny baby. We give our verbal consent on the understanding that someone will call us as soon as Sean has recovered.

For the second time that day I break down in tears and Darron slams about the kitchen. We are both incensed and upset, as Mark, too young to understand what is going on, climbs up on my knee. I sit there cuddling one son and thinking of the other. Sean is less than two hours away, but he might as well have been on another continent.

CHAPTER 8.

A member of staff from the hospital confirms Sean has recovered well from the anaesthetic and she informs me that he is on the mental health ward, giving me directions on how to get there. She puts me at ease a little by telling me that the nurses from the hospital have sent his clothes and the breast milk that I had already expressed, that had been stored in the freezer at Stepping Hill Hospital. I feel at least they will take care of him and we will drive to the hospital in the morning.

On Sunday 1st February we are still unable to get to Manchester and so Darron and I attend church. We each make a call to the hospital, Darron in the morning and me in the afternoon, but we are told nothing. It is the day after when we finally make it through the snow to the hospital, now desperate to see our sick baby son.

Where we live in Buxton, Derbyshire, snow is not unusual. In fact, only this last year, we have had record amounts. Often the snow is so localised that we can leave home in snow boots and winter coats and arrive in Stockport, forty minutes later, to only an inch or two. Some friends who visited us in late January parked their car outside the house in a space we had cleared and the snow surrounding the car was higher than the bonnet. It impressed them so much they took photos to show their friends and family back in Birmingham. I don't really think some of the staff from Manchester realise what winters are like in the Derbyshire hills or even how hard it is for us to get to the city.

A specialist nurse from Manchester Children's Hospital recently came to my son's school to talk to staff about another child's medical condition. When she finally arrived forty-five minutes late, she declared that we would have to get a specialist nurse from the Children's Hospital near to us in future. She was shocked to discover that she *was* from the nearest Children's Hospital.

On Monday 2nd February I speak to Karen, our Health Visitor, and fill her in on what has been happening. She calls the hospital for us and assures us that we *will* speak to a doctor when we arrive. We arrive at the hospital and enter the main building asking for the mental health ward and quickly ascertain that the 'ward' is a separate building across the car park from the shiny bright main entrance.

Darron and I go through a dark hallway into the single storey building and ask the nearest nurse for news. She introduces herself as Pat, the ward sister, she is short, portly and stern and she gives us no further information as to how Sean is doing. We hear a baby crying constantly and immediately we recognise it as Sean. The sound is muffled, but distinctly audible, it sounds distant and we look around for his cot.

As we are shown past the nurses' station to the opposite end of the ward there is a small room with barred windows on the outside and windows in the room that look out onto the ward. It dawns on us that Sean couldn't have been further from the watchful gaze of the staff. In fact, in the room where the nurses all sit chatting and discussing cases you could have barely heard a crying baby through a closed door at the other end of the ward. We hear him easily as we open the door and are greeted with a shocking sight.

Sean has been without us for two days as we had struggled to get through the snow. A dummy lies in his cot but it isn't his. A bottle of formula sits on the work surface at the side next to him but he should be breastfed. His clothes had been minimal due to monitors and canulas (he had only been able to wear short dungarees since his first admission – we went out and bought them especially so that he would look 'dressed') but he isn't wearing any of them.

All Sean wears is a cotton smock, stained and dirty-looking and a soiled nappy. I comment dryly that if he was found like that at home Social Services would have him removed, a comment that would turn out to be somewhat prophetic.

We realise that despite the fact that there are posters detailing parental access to children's medical notes, Sean's notes are not present. All there is in the room is a feeding chart and in the back of this chart is a leaflet about the dangers of X-rays on young children and babies. I read it in the absence of anything more relevant, passing the time and in a bid to educate myself out of genuine interest. We are told nothing about the findings of the MRI scan and assume that the results are not back, the reaction of medical staff on the ward seems somewhat cool if not a little icy.

The following day, we bring Mark to see his brother again and we spend some time in the playroom. I spot a box full of baby mobiles on top of a cupboard and I ask the ward sister, Pat, if I can borrow one for Sean's cot. I am briskly told there is no point in providing him with a mobile as, with his medical findings, he will be unable to see it. I am shocked and cross, I know nothing of any findings and having been kept in the dark for two days I counter: "Well he certainly won't be able to see it on top of the cupboard!"

A young nurse who hears the exchange offers to get the box down and I win a small victory as Darron attaches it to Sean's cot. He looks significantly worse since transferring from Stepping Hill Hospital and some of the staff appear to watch us like hawks. For the first time an uneasy feeling creeps over me but I can't work out what it relates to. I would like to claim at least a decent level of intelligence and the hackles on my neck are standing on end as I discuss with Darron the absence of notes and the absence of any information.

I chat to other mums in the parent room and make idle small talk. I see one mum and dad spend time wrapping rope lights around their little girl's cot, taking time to ensure they cover every bar. Their daughter is older than Sean, but younger than Mark. I estimate that she is probably somewhere between twelve and eighteen months of age. I watch them mainly for something to do and, as they stand aside, I see that their daughter is severely disabled. I wonder if that will be us in a years time and wonder what caused the brain damage that now means she doesn't sit up or try to talk.

As I continue to watch I can't help but smile as the parents proudly turn on the lights, I am mesmerised by this act of love and the interest the little girl shows in the lights as they run in waves, twinkling around the cold metal bars of the cot. The parents spend some time with their daughter and then talk to the nurses briefly before leaving for the day.

I question myself as I consider how we are going to cope with any disability Sean might have and I resolve to be like those parents, who were trying to do their best in every way possible to improve their daughter's life. I also see first hand when Pat, the ward sister, strides over to the cot minutes after the parents leave and switches off the lights stating loudly: "What a waste of electricity! Nothing will come of this child, I don't know why they can't accept it." Bile rises in my throat as anger surges through me. I want to shout at her, to ask why she ever became a nurse, but I am stopped by the doctor bringing news that Sean is to be sent for a skeletal x-ray and a scan on his heart.

The heart scan takes place almost immediately in the coronary department across the car park. As I pick Sean up and wrap him in a blanket I am told by a nurse that I am not allowed to carry Sean, he will have to go in a pram. A pram is eventually found to travel the short distance across the car park but I have no idea why a pram is required.

The scene feels odd and I ask the nurse why I can't carry him. The nurse, slender and not overly tall with dark hair, keeps walking and then asks me if anyone has mentioned N.A.I. to us. I reply that they haven't and as we arrive outside the scan room she looks at me for the first time and says, "I'm sure it will be alright then."

Vexed by her cryptic statement I ponder her meaning as the cardiologist turns off the lights and scans Sean's heart. He makes no small talk or conversation, eventually handing me an Endocarditis Warning Card and informing me that Sean has a hole in his heart. That is it. No information, no leaflet, no more news. A follow-up appointment is handed to me and I am accompanied by the nurse as I push my son back to the ward.

I don't recall the name of the nurse, just that she was fairly young and dark haired. It is ironic really as she was the only nurse who in our time there had showed compassion. It was her who had helped me to obtain the mobile for Sean's cot and as we near the end of our absurdly short journey back to the mental health unit, it is her who tells me the staff at Pendlebury are on edge. I ask her why, sensing that there is a lot more to tell, and her voice drops. She stands still, wavering slightly, just outside the entrance to the ward. She looks over her shoulder and then through the doors to the ward and I can't help but suspect she isn't supposed to be mentioning whatever information she has.

Her whisper is quiet but it is like a bomb has gone off in my head: the staff had seen a similar case and as they had no evidence of abuse they had decided to the send the baby home…the baby had later been found dead.

I felt sick. Sick that someone could do that to a baby, sick that we could possibly be compared to a child abuser, sick that we would pay for the backlash of suspicion that would fall on other parents who had done nothing but their best. They would not let us home easily, backs would be covered, we would be watched and they would be determined not to risk making the same mistake again. Whatever we did or said would never be enough if the hospital staff were determined to protect themselves from any possible retribution by claiming guilt regardless of evidence.

I convey what I have been told to Darron, who is waiting by Sean's cot. We ask when the skeletal x-ray is due to take place and we are told that a card has been sent to the department but no appointment time has been given. We wait and then wait some more. At 1.00p.m. We tell the nursing staff that we are going to grab some lunch in the café so that if an appointment comes through they can let us know.

By sheer luck we arrive back on the ward just in time to accompany Sean; nobody had come to find us. On our arrival at the x-ray department we ask if x-rays are dangerous and are told that they are perfectly safe. I would think that most people know and are aware of the dangers of radiation; they know that x-rays whilst pregnant can be damaging and, as parents, Darron and I had both read of the dangers in the only leaflet that had been left with Sean's feeding chart.

Whilst the hospital staff declare the safety of the x-rays we are asked to stand behind a screen. It doesn't take an expert to know we are being lied to. I know something isn't right and I am sure that there is a major cloud hanging over us - I just don't know why. Whilst numerous x-rays of every part of our newborn baby's body take place I see a chart above the protective screen we are standing behind.

It is simple flowchart - a step by step guide on determining non-accidental injuries. A small box has the question: *Could the injury have been non-accidental?* Two lines leading in different directions from the box have the words *yes* and *no*. The *yes* box is followed by large bold red print stating *refer to Social Services.* I wonder how many injuries you could fit into that box and how you can tell from an x-ray how an injury is caused. That however isn't the problem of the medical professionals: they refer the case and trust social workers to assess the difference between the abusive and non-abusive cases by using their own professional opinion.

Darron, Sean and I are all back on the ward a short while later when Dr. Helen Williams and a nurse called Stephanie greet us, inviting us to join them in a meeting room.

Dr. Williams tells us of her preliminary findings, namely that:

- The CT scan taken at Stepping Hill Hospital and placed on top of Sean's incubator in the ambulance is missing.
- There is what she believes to be an old subdural bleed, possibly relating to birth.
- There is a new bleed of unknown origin.
- An opinion from Dr. Fieldman raises the possibility of N.A.I. (non-accidental injury)

Dr. Williams adds that she has worked with Dr. Fieldman for many years and has never known him to give such a "hazy opinion". There is no time scale to the bleeds and Dr. Fieldman has gone to London. There is a possibility of the bleeds happening whilst Sean has been in hospital but she is unsure.

Darron and I tell Dr. Williams of the state we had found Sean in and the care we believe is lacking. She promises to do all she can to rectify the situation and Dr. Williams tells us that she does not yet feel the need to contact Social Services but that she will await the results of an ophthalmology assessment and the skeletal x-rays.

In all the time she talks tears stream down my face. I ask her how the injury can be non-accidental if there are no bruises or external injuries and for the first time the theory of shaking is mentioned. I get up and leave the room in blind rage. How dare they? After all they have done or failed to do, how dare they point the finger at us!

I watch Darron leave the meeting room and come over to me by Sean's cot. We look into each other's eyes but nothing needs to be said, we know how the other feels, we know why we have been shunned and kept in the dark. The cloud we were under was suspicion.

Much later as Dr. Williams comes back with the results of the eye examination she enters the room but does not look at us. She stares out of the window as she tells us: "As everyone expected the x-rays were clear, adding; but you already knew that." I catch her eye as she turns but she looks down at the floor as if she finds the conversation difficult. Dr. Williams talks further mentioning that there are some tiny haemorrhages behind the eyes that have most probably been present since birth and are of no significant importance.

It still means nothing to me as I struggle to comprehend why any of this is relevant to Sean's current wellbeing. I add in almost a flippant tone "This may sound stupid to you but could you actually tell us how Sean is?" She reassures me that my request is not stupid, as I already know it isn't, and for the first time we are brought up to date with Sean's progress.

Today, years after, I can feel for her predicament. I know that her job rests on the fact that she will follow the flowchart, that she must protect herself by referring the matter to Social Services and that she feels that there is no evidence of abuse. To her credit she does not lie. She tells us that she will have to speak to Social Services, but adds that in cases like ours, with no real evidence, it will probably mean a letter on file.

I have wondered since if she was comforting herself by this thought. She also discussed the option of obtaining a second opinion on the scan findings as non-accidental injury seemed such an unlikely explanation. I would later reflect on the possibility that it was her who would obtain the report from Dr. Timmin, a report that would become so controversial.

We ask Dr. Williams to transfer Sean back to Stepping Hill to make travelling easier and, although neither Darron nor I say it, in order to get the care we feel Sean needs and deserves. We listen to her instruct Sister Pat to check bed availability and arrange transport as soon as possible but due to the limited transport available Sister Pat ventures that it will be the following morning before the transfer can take place.

Darron and I travel home shell-shocked consoled only by the thought that it will be easier to drive back to Stockport in the morning. I had not been staying the previous few nights at the hospital, as the attitude of the staff was so poor towards both of us and I was struggling to cope.

CHAPTER 9.

On Tuesday 3rd February we travel from home to Stepping Hill Hospital to meet Sean's ambulance from Pendlebury and at 1.00p.m. We call the ward at Manchester Children's hospital to find out if the ambulance has definitely left. Sister Pat comes on the phone to notify us that the transfer has not been finalised. The staff at Stepping Hill have been waiting for him to arrive all morning and are surprised to learn that Sean is still in the care of the hospital in Manchester. By 4.30p.m. when the transfer is no nearer to taking place, we call the ward at Manchester again. Sister Pat's voice, monotonous, conveys no emotion as she tells us the transfer will take place in the next day or so.

Having felt under immense pressure for the previous few weeks we are at our wits end. Darron and I have constantly been left in the dark and misled. Despite Dr. Williams's assurances that the transfer would be straight forward and virtually immediate, not one person could tell us why it had still not taken place. The tone of the ward sister as she spoke to us was harsh and unfeeling, we were guilty pure and simple. We did not deserve our son; we were cold hearted child abusers who were to be treated like pariahs.

Darron picks up the phone shortly after with the sole intention of finding out what is going on. He speaks to an unnamed nurse who transmits repeated messages from the ward sister who refuses to come to the phone. I pick up the phone from him and ask to speak to Sister Pat in person and, after a lengthy pause, she picks up the phone huffing. I ask why the transfer has not been sorted and I am told it has not been authorised.

Fed up with the repeated run around I demand Dr. Helen Williams's direct line, only to be suddenly told the problem is down to a breakdown in communication and he will be transferred shortly. I tersely thank her for her 'help' and request that we are kept informed. Pat calls back at 8.30p.m. to tell us that the first ambulance available will be the following morning and we ask to be called again so that we can meet Sean there.

Wednesday morning arrives slowly as we go through the motions, dressing Mark and making him breakfast. It has been a while now since either Darron or I felt like eating. I had lost a complete dress size in recent weeks and food just didn't hold any appeal. Mark was aware that things were different but his cheeky smile helped to keep us going. I was made acutely aware how Mark perceived his new sibling when I heard him talking to his little friend Jacob one day. As they played on the small slide in the garden I overheard him tell his playmate that he had a new brother but that we kept him at the hospital for safe keeping. Out of the mouths of babes.

The phone's shrill ring breaks the tension and we both dive for the receiver. Darron gets there first and relays the message that Sean's ambulance leaves at 10.00a.m. We'd had many long discussions about the fact that if he was transferred to Stepping Hill it was a step closer to bringing him home and we grasp the news with enthusiasm. Upon his arrival at Stepping Hill Hospital we are given the first detailed update on his condition, which is much improved and stable. Darron asks if he will be able to come home soon but the staff are slightly evasive, only telling us that the consultant is on his way.

Dr. Fearn arrives at 5.00p.m. and for the first time since we met him his face looks grave. Dr. Fieldman can only offer trauma as the explanation for the injury as there is no other explanation he can think of. Dr. Fieldman would later provide evidence in another case that led to the removal of a child from its parents for over a year before the judge pointed out how Fieldman had used language which was 'too absolute' in relation to the possible cause of the baby's alleged injuries, later attributed to oxygen starvation in the womb.

In the meantime we are told that the findings are not consistent with anything in particular and Dr. Helen Williams and Dr. Fearn have discussed the fact that neither of them think this is a case of N.A.I. (non-accidental injury). We again ask for clarification of non-accidental injury and the only word ventured is from a nurse who quietly adds 'shaking'.

Dr. Fearn informs us that Social Services have already been contacted and a case officer will be assigned. Despite all the feelings from those professionals who have spoken to us, we are told that the only thing they can do now is to try to limit the damage an investigation will cause. No Emergency Protection Order has been applied for and nobody directly accuses us of anything. Sean can come home as soon as everything has been agreed with the case worker.

On Thursday 5th February, we have been waiting at the hospital for a meeting with the consultant. By 4.20p.m. we are advised that he is running late and that Social Services have yet to give permission for Sean to go home. At 5.10p.m. there is still no news as a nurse comes to check on Sean, chatting amicably to us, telling us about her own daughter and about cases that happened in the hospital she worked at previously.

The nurse administers Sean's medicine and talks openly, telling us that none of the ward staff are surprised by "all of this". I ask what she means and she states that there are some hospitals that are much keener to blame parents than others. She offers that the Children's Hospital in Pendlebury, Manchester, has a reputation with the staff at Stepping Hill for their regularity and eagerness to apportion blame. As she talks she tells us of other hospitals she had worked at and how one other was also known for the frequency of non-accidental injury findings.

As she takes off her apron and washes her hands she fills in Sean's notes and I see that after the end of each line there have been lines drawn to the end of the page. I ask why this is the case, this is the first time we have seen Sean's notes since he had been transferred initially and I had never seen the staff draw the lines on before. The almost guilty look was familiar, I had seen it with the nurse who had told me about the recent death at Pendlebury, an edginess and reluctance to speak out of turn but an eagerness to be honest and truthful. What she said next shocked me to the core.

"We have noticed, some of the nursing staff here I mean, that things seem to have been...added to the notes. Some of the writing is squeezed in and one of the nurses knows, well I mean to say...she always uses the same pen you see." It took me a minute, the cogs in my mind whirring, before I could stutter: "They've changed his notes?" Her bobbed blonde hair covered her face as she nodded and continued, "Be careful, they cover their own backs first. Keep a diary, write in it everything anyone says, go home and write down everything you remember whilst you remember it."

As she left the room my mind was still spinning. Darron was pacing up and down chuntering in a mixture of disbelief and anger. Our resentment towards the system was growing daily and now it seemed that even some of the professionals could not be trusted.

We talked in hushed tones with an urgency to our conversation. How could we check what was in the notes and how would we, as lay people, know what had been there and what might have been added? The more we thought about it, the more it seemed ludicrous. Still, the next time we nipped to the shops I bought a notebook and started writing.

CHAPTER 10.

When we finally speak to Dr. Fearn he looks tired and weary. God knows how many hours he has been working. On top of trying to treat patients and save the lives of very sick children he has liaised with social workers, provided reports and, as would happen in our case, attended case conferences. He smiles wanly as he relays the information he has ascertained from Social Services: Sean could not be allowed home until after a strategy meeting on Monday. He advises us that nobody stands accused of anything but everyone must be seen to do their job. I ask him what happens if we discharge Sean ourselves and I recoil as he replies: "The police will have to be called".

We are told that our contact at Social Services will be a social worker called Andrea. I obtain her number, or rather the number of the 'on duty' call desk, and travel home to start making calls. I am sure that this misunderstanding will pass once they have visited us, have seen our home and have met our eldest son, Mark. Two of the nurses also stop us on our way out of the ward to tell us that the situation is 'ridiculous' but they are sure it will 'soon be ironed out'.

As we leave the hospital Darron is stopped by a sister from the ward who insists that none of the staff on the site believe we injured Sean in any way. The support is uplifting but it only compounds our disbelief that we are in our present situation. Throughout everything we are constantly given nuggets of support and reassuring phrases only for them to be worth nothing when it counts.

As 9.00a.m. on Friday comes around I phone the

number I have been given for Social Services reception. I have been walking around the house with the phone in my hand, egging the clock on as if time would somehow move faster and now I feel nervous but determined. Andrea answers the phone in a gentle and calm voice, disarming me immediately. I ask her why the meeting is scheduled for Monday and not today instead and apparently this is so my obstetrician can attend.

We knew that the obstetrician had spoken to Karen, our health visitor, previously. He told her that some of the changes seen on the scan could be due to birth trauma and we hoped that he would soon tell Social Services the same thing.

Andrea tells me that we will have to wait for Monday's meeting in order for Social Services to make a plan of action, up until then there will be no way of knowing how long Sean will be prevented from returning home. I beg her to come and meet us, insisting that we have nothing to hide. She lets me finish before advising me that they have no right to be involved whilst a medical cause could still be found. I wonder why, if there is no right to any involvement, our son is incarcerated against our will.

I ask her what will happen if the medical evidence does not support us. Andrea pauses and stresses that *if* no alternative explanation can be found, Sean will go to foster care or pending assessment, extended family whilst an investigation is undertaken. I ask if we will be represented at this meeting but the answer is no, this is a professionals meeting and not a case conference. Months later, when questions arose as to the origin of the report that changed our lives, nobody would admit that the professionals meeting took place.

As I finish the call I suddenly feel the exhaustion that has been plaguing me for weeks. Darron had started to experience severe pains in his lower back and side and was now passing blood in his urine. My hair was falling out in clumps, my skin was peeling and, as my weight dropped away my milk was drying up. We were very short of sleep and struggling to keep up the pretence of normality to those who were not in our immediate family. We were sure that the situation was temporary and we were too busy travelling to and from the hospital to speak to friends. I suddenly felt isolated, I didn't know anyone this had happened to and I didn't know how to help myself.

I picked up the phone again and spoke to Karen and as I began to explain the situation she interjects. Her immense support and determination to fight the case on our behalf is the best thing I have heard in weeks. She goes on to assure me that they will be sending representation to the meeting on Monday and that every person that could be involved on our behalf, will be involved, including our GP. I feel my spirits lift. If all these people believe us, surely there would be no grounds to keep Sean from coming home.

Over the weekend we keep up the round of visiting Sean and playing with Mark. Sean is improving but still seems very sleepy as the phenobarbitone is keeping him sedated. We hear more history from a nurse called Paula, who had been on duty the day Sean was due to be transferred. She asks what happened and what caused the delay, as staff at Stepping Hill had been constantly calling to chase the transfer. They, like us, had no idea what the delay had been.

Mark's second birthday is in a matter of days and we have not yet bought him a present. Whilst in Stockport we take the opportunity to shop for a birthday gift for Mark and a 'welcome home' gift for Sean. Walking through one shop I see a fluffy teddy bear face with a cloth attached; little paws and feet at each corner. I fall in love with it instantly and can't wait to give it to Sean. 'Flopsy', as we named it, remains to this day one of his most prized possessions.

The day of the meeting, Monday 9th February, arrives. We visit Sean in the morning and then return home to await a phone call with the outcome of the meeting. My parents have phoned already but we have no news, we are all distressed. A call not long after 5.00p.m., from a social worker, tells us that we will be reunited with Sean within twenty-four hours, as soon as discharge paperwork and medication can be arranged. The social worker, Mary Howard, informs us that Dr. Fearn will tell us more but that there will be a family support meeting to offer us support after everything we have been through.

It's over. Sean will be home for Mark's birthday on February 11th. We can start our life as a family of four. I write thank you letters to staff on the ward, Dr. Williams and Dr. Fearn and deliver them to the hospital. I am elated and for the first time in months I fall asleep as soon as my head hits the pillow. Thank God.

CHAPTER 11.

On Tuesday the 10th February we are contacted by our newly appointed Social worker, Mary Howard. Mary is slight in stature with red hair and wearing a denim jacket and jeans. I estimate her age to be above forty, but perhaps not yet over fifty. Darron, Mark and I are all present for her visit and after making cups of tea I join them in the living room.

The first thing Mary hands me is a copy of the complaints procedure, which I find somewhat odd. I ask her when Sean can come home and she replies that decision is to be taken by the doctors. despite the fact that we have been told by the doctors that the decision will be taken by Social Services. Mary Howard claims she is unaware that is the case and that she must speak to the hospital staff with a view to straightening out the misunderstanding.

Mary asks us how we are coping and we reply that we are much better for the knowledge that Sean will soon be home. She nods courteously and continues to watch Mark run endlessly up and down the hall with his cement mixer. She smiles a little as he comes over and babbles to her singing 'Bob the Builder', putting the cement mixer down momentarily in order to clap to his song. He turns to his Dad for more adulation, sure that his entertainment will be rewarded with praise, which Darron bestows.

Mary talks while we try to ascertain why she is here. As far as we were led to believe there were no other concerns about Sean; the doctors and nursing staff didn't believe we harmed him. Yet, here in our living room, sits a social worker. The question goes unasked for some time, as we chat amicably, until I eventually need to know; "What is the purpose of your visit?" She looks almost relieved as she reaches into a bag and starts pulling out bits of paper.

As her lips move I can feel that I am distancing myself. This isn't over; my mind tries to quickly work out scenarios as in vain I try to figure out what will happen next. Finally she finishes repeating the medical history we have given so many times over the previous weeks and adds; "I'm not sure in what capacity I'm here. I don't yet know if I am here for 'child protection' or 'supporting families'." Comfortingly she adds "Quite often when young children have been so seriously ill, we are asked to come and offer some kind of support."

Darron and I never question the explanation, we know after all that Sean is completely safe with us, we have never and would never hurt him. We automatically assume that she must be here to offer us support in the aftermath of everything. Looking back we are exceptionally naïve. As she details the concern raised from the scan findings and talks about non-accidental injury we constantly counter her with all the medical findings that have not been investigated. We try to remain calm but state our case firmly as she re-iterates that the report merely states a 'possibility'.

Mary has called her line manager and informs us that she has reiterated to him: "They aren't the normal kind of family I see". Seeing Darron look a little confused I imagine that my look is similar. How bizarre, how very strange, now I know what they mean about social workers I think to myself. Thanking her for her time we show her out. Stepping out the door she turns and glances back before saying: "You have a lovely home." I smile fleetingly and in my mind I answer: I know.

The ward staff call us early the same afternoon to tell us Sean is ready to be discharged. We call at the shop to pick up a gift of chocolates and a bottle of sparkling wine for Dr. Fearn. To this day we will always be eternally grateful to him for saving our son. As a doctor he helped to save Sean's life and as a human being he showed empathy and compassion, ensuring that our son could stay in hospital until Social Services were prepared to let him home. It is medical professionals like him that use their own judgement, that put their own necks on the line to do whatever they believe is best for their patient.

We pull up in the hospital car park at around 3.00p.m. as Mary Howard telephones Darron's mobile to tell us she will visit us again at 4.00p.m.. Knowing that the return journey will take at least forty-five minutes we know we haven't much time as we deliver the thank you letters and cards and strap Sean into his car seat, picking up his large bag of medication whilst receiving a constant flow of nursing staff who have come to say goodbye.

It takes us more than forty-five minutes to get home to our village and as we walk through the door I become conscious of the fact that the house feels strange. I have spent so little time here in recent weeks and the post is neatly stacked on top of the work surface. The car ride has worked its magic on both the children, who are now sound asleep. I carry Sean in to his home in his car seat and Darron lifts the unusually sleepy Mark into his cot.

It wasn't normal for Mark to have a daytime nap; I was always quite envious of other mums who settle down in the afternoon to catch up on housework and washing or maybe even read a book in peace. I feel limbless. I have no idea what to do next. Our lives have been so hectic. In the hospital there had always been lights and sounds, people going about their jobs at all hours and now there is utter silence.

I open the post, mainly out of a need for a sense of purpose. The bills have been mounting whilst we struggled to keep all the plates spinning. Darron, who had never shown the slightest interest in the finances, looks a little sheepish as he explains that he has left them for me. I understand immediately, he is useless with money, even today he will buy the children an endless stream of gifts given half a chance, without a thought to the bank balance. We share money equally and, at different times, we have each earned more and less than each other. It is swings and roundabouts. I have a nice comfortable home and my children have more than enough toys to play a whole month without repeat.

Despite this my children, like most other children, have firm favourites. The old faithfuls come out time and again, with others seeing the light of day only briefly, when friend's come to play. I try to keep a reign on Darron's generous nature but he knows deep down I would spend every penny quite happily on 'my boys'. I use that phrase to cover the whole family often telling people I have three children, but only two under ten!

Post marriage, Darron had insisted that the dog we both wanted would be male, he claimed that otherwise he would be outnumbered. One male dog, two male guinea pigs, two boys and a husband later I ask him how he could possibly be outnumbered? He replies with a grin and just out of reach: "You're a woman – they always get the deciding vote!"

Darron and I have barely got into the house with both of the children when the social worker arrives. Her tone has changed from earlier in the day and she now dictates that we will be subject to regular visits from Social Services. We try to remain calm as we ascertain why these visits have not been mentioned in any of the calls we have had with her previously. Darron requests to know who decides such things as I bombard her with the factors that we believe have a part in why Sean has had a brain hemorrhage.

We are told for the first time that she didn't know what was happening, a phrase that would oft be repeated as she tells us that until after she had spoken to her line manager she didn't know what capacity she was involved with us. The shock barely takes the edge off the horrifying statement that failure to comply with the 'request' would result in both the children being removed.

So it was that we spent the first night at home together as a family in weeks. We read Mark stories, cuddle Sean to sleep and lay him down in his Tigger-filled nursery. Mark slowly creeps in before getting in to his own bed and reaches through the cot bars whispering "Night, night Shawny" and my life feels complete again. The large cloud looming over us feels like it will pass - after all, we have nothing to hide.

The following day we celebrate Mark's birthday and enjoy being a family of four. We stroll through the park with the dog and people we know, and strangers, take the opportunity to coo into the pram and declare how like his dad Sean is, in the usual fashion. For the most part Mark runs around throwing sticks for the dog. Mac, our white West Highland Terrier, runs about picking them up only inches from Mark's boots where they have been 'thrown', the dog tosses them high in the air playing happily. The snow is still visible on the hilltops and there is a way to go until spring, the air is cold but fresh.

As we push the pram home and get to the door, the phone is already ringing. Mary Howard has called to tell us she will be visiting again the next day and after agreeing a time she hangs up. "What was that all about?" Darron asked as he wiped the dog's paws. "I'm not really sure." I reply, still failing to get a grasp on the situation.

Mary Howard would later record that our home and safety of our children is of a high standard. That we are 'emotionally warm' and that Mark's development and ability is excellent. It goes on record that we are co-operating but not the reason why. Even at this early stage there are undertones of what might happen if N.A.I., an acronym for shaken baby syndrome is 'proved'. I am told in no uncertain terms that Mark is the one who has rescued his brother. Mark's good behaviour, happy disposition and advanced ability for his age — at two he can already name colours and had started to name a few letters — means that they could not suggest that we aren't good parents.

It is unthinkable to imagine what would have happened if Sean had been our first child. We wouldn't have been any more likely to be abusive or violent towards him but we would have no evidence to prove it. Already we have to prove our innocence. As Mark runs about playing and relishing the extra visitor's attention I feel a powerful rush of maternal love towards my eldest son, the brother who would save Sean not once, but twice.

On the 13th February 2004, a third home visit takes place with more professionals involved. I am introduced to two people from the family support service who will be a part of the so-called protection plan. Caroline and Nicola are openly warm and very light-hearted in the way they speak. I can tell that they are used to dealing with both parents and children in a daily capacity.

Caroline's attention is focused entirely on Mark, chatting away with the usual high pitched sing-songy voice normally reserved for small children. She praises him often and encourages him to 'build' with his blocks and play set, which means he makes a lot of very loud tapping and hammering noises throughout the meeting.

Darron and I are introduced to them both as support workers offering their help after a long and difficult time for us. We recognise that this support is not voluntary and raise many questions, wanting to know where we stand and why they are harming our family with such intrusive behaviour. I am answered clearly and with a low authorative tone, reminiscent of Supernanny; "You have your children...we *are* helping you."

It would be the first of many occasions when I was made to feel like the children are my special reward for co-operation. I was an unknown entity not to be trusted: they are the experts in the field and the one's who knew what was best for my children. The threats are veiled but the gloves are soon to come off.

On the 19th and 20th February Mary Howard visits again, alone this time, after making several phone calls. Mary advises me that the verbal report from Dr. Timmin is 'not good news' and that if Darron or myself can't come up with a good enough explanation of Sean's injury our children will be taken away. It became normal that upon each visit she would recite this 'new evidence' in the form of more bits of paper. In fact in the whole case there would never be any more evidence. Simply the same statements made by different neuroradiologists and the reluctance of laypeople, not versed in medical findings, to raise their heads above the parapet.

The possibility of a non-accidental injury was mentioned repeatedly but nobody seemed to take any of our concerns or issues further. The family support workers who had been introduced to us under the guise of helping us after the traumatic time we had, started a parenting assessment, whilst the social worker, Mary Howard failed to start the core assessment at all.

The visits are increasing in frequency as, on occasion, Caroline, Nicola and Mary Howard arrive at different times, the visits interspersed with phone calls and updates. The updates generally result in Darron or me being told that things are 'not looking good'. The main thread is simply that despite over ten different causes and contributory factors being put forward the medical professionals (neuroradiologists) are not moving from a deliberate shaking injury.

Our own health visitor, Karen, and Gina, the play worker from the local health centre, are also involved in visiting us on a regular basis but both Karen and Gina' visits provide welcome relief from the accusatory and forceful tone which Mary Howard is now adopting.

The following week goes in a blur of visits and assessment. We are visited on average three times a day and

---

called at least twice. I start trawling the yellow pages for solicitors who will be able to help us and we meet several. Some merely state that legal representation is needed for court but is ineffective. Social Services, it seems, will do what they feel best and everyone else will have to toe the line. One solicitor even tells us that in all his cases the outcome was virtually decided when the case first went to court and that almost none of the additional evidence he found or presented was likely to make the slightest difference as the medical professionals hid behind each other.

We walk down the steep, eroded stone steps from his office determined that he is wrong. We both state that there is no way we will instruct him, he was clearly no good at his job or so we assumed. As it turned out, he was right.

As the end of February approaches we are informed by telephone that there will be a case conference held for Sean. We have no idea why there is a sudden need for a conference, or what it means. We are given a photocopied leaflet detailing what a case conference is in bubbly, friendly speak with simple to read phrasing. Darron and I are advised that the meeting is a chance to participate and put our views, in fact if we so desire we can submit a parental statement. The meeting will discuss and decide on whether our children are at risk of injury from us, taking into consideration all the factors and all the views of those who will be attending.

I work on our submission for days, eventually handing in a paper that runs to seventeen pages. I mention all the factors I have found that contribute to subdural haematomas in other cases, the failings in Sean's care initially and a stack of evidence to show that subdural haematomas can even be found in a baby in the womb or in babies who had only ever been in hospital. I feel confident that I can show that there are many factors that could either explain a subdural haematoma or mean that it becomes more likely.

I was aided in my quest for knowledge by researching on the Internet. I quickly come across a support group called

---

80

'The Five Percenters', their name derived from the estimated five percent of parents who are wrongly accused of Shaken Baby Syndrome. They detail case histories that read like a nightmarish list of the ill-fated. They are us and we are them. I call the founder and campaigner who runs the group, Rioch Edwards-Brown. As I tell her what I know about our case she tells me what will happen next. I confess to being sceptical; that won't happen to us I think to myself, we have lots of medical professionals on our side.

I call again in the run-up to the case conference and she questions me further about the case history, checking that the skeletal survey had been clear and asking about our other son. I realise that in order to help us she had to be clear in her own mind that we are in fact one of the five percent, not an abusive or neglectful parent who may choose to turn to others to get them out of a bad situation. Rioch advises me to get decent legal representation and warns me of the numbers of solicitors who follow almost a pro-forma in these cases, failing to put before the court vital evidence. Prior to hanging up the phone she simply adds "Welcome home".

The last days in February are spent taking phone calls and receiving visits from Mary Howard. Her constant insinuation is that any explanation for Sean's injury is better than none. Hours go by as she determinedly questions us over and over, barely allowing us time to function as parents at all, insisting that we must have forgotten something. She seems to get increasingly frustrated that we fail to confess and she constantly repeats the threat that this will mean the removal of the children.

CHAPTER 12.

The case conference has been scheduled but we are told that Sean's paediatrician, GP and Health Visitor will not be able to attend. Darron makes several phone calls to ask Dr. Fearn, the GP and Karen to submit letters and reports for the meeting instead. It transpires that none of them know the meeting is still to go ahead. Things start to look a little odd. I make a call to Mary Howard only to be told that she is busy on another call, I insist on holding the line, listening to some tuneless single note music until I finally hear her voice.

Mary states her name and her post as a social worker but I can wait no longer launching straight in with "Why did the doctor's not know the case conference was going ahead?" She pauses before informing me that the decision on whether the children are to be registered as 'at risk' will not take place at this initial conference. I counter that surely all professionals should be given the option to attend, nevertheless she states that that's the way things are, not forgetting to add another off-hand remark about the fact that we are 'lucky enough' to have our children.

The case conference takes place on the 2nd March 2004. Prior to the meeting Mary Howard encourages us to bring the children with us advising us that the other professionals would like to see them at the conference. My parents, Darron and I had all decided against this. We didn't know what the outcome of the meeting was likely to be and our guard was up. There was even talk that if the children went to the meeting they could be removed from there, as we were now so convinced that something had gone wrong, we just didn't know what.

I dress in a suit carrying several copies of my parental submission with me. I am determined that whatever happens I am going to state my case. Upon signing in at Social Services reception, the lady at the front desk offers us tea and shows us in to the meeting. We have barely got through the door when we are ushered out and in to a small side room. It transpires that the professionals are having a brief chat first.

From the way I was dressed, in a navy suit, the receptionist had assumed I was a professional attending the meeting and had made the mistake of letting me in. Due to this error, I had been able to see that coffee cups and tea cups were already on the table, the meeting had in fact already started — we, however, were still not allowed through.

Mary Howard comes to fetch us a short time later, seemingly surprised by the lack of our children. We state that we have left them in the capable hands of their grandparents. As she leads us back through the security door she advises us that a further report on Sean's MRI scan had been received by Dr. Timmin. The news is of the worst kind. Dr. Timmin has concluded that although some of the changes on the brain scan could have been caused from birth, the bleeding in the brain is traumatic and has happened since. The final line of the report merely concludes that there is a possibility of non-accidental injury.

There hasn't been time, we are told, to get a copy of the report to everyone prior to the meeting so everyone is still reading it. I ask if the conference can be delayed to allow everyone, including ourselves, chance to read it and, in our case, defend ourselves against it. Mary Howard merely states that there is no time available, we must all "Skip to the conclusions of the report". It is the first of many occasions where the timing is last minute and where information isn't circulated to all parties. Everyone is expected to make decisions based on a brief appraisal provided by Mary Howard.

Reports from each of the people present are provided and, despite the best efforts of our social worker, Mary Howard, the meeting is attended by Nicola and Caroline from Social Services family support, Dr. Fearn (Sean's Paediatrician), Karen (our Health Visitor), our GP, and a local police officer, Darron and myself. The police officer present confirms that neither of us has ever been arrested and that we are not known to the police in any way and our Health Visitor and GP continue to re-iterate that they have no concerns.

The family support workers present their reports containing detail of our positive parenting and for the most part, keep quiet. Dr. Fearn can do nothing other than show the scans and state that he has no other opinion on them as he isn't an expert in the field. We sit and listen to people discussing our lives and our children.

Karen had become a great source of support, as had our GP, who writes a report for the case conference asking the very question that would years later become so relevant "Was Sean at a greater risk of bleeding and had full investigations been carried out with regards to this?" I can only surmise that in fact the answer was no.

Whatever the medical professionals offer as possible cause or reason to investigate further is belittled by the social worker and Chair of the meeting as being barely relevant. They are there to protect the children and that means adding their names on to the child protection register. Darron eventually leaves the room distressed as a vote is started, a vote on whether or not our children are at risk and need to be put on the register.

As the Chairperson seeks the votes from around the table, the social worker and family support workers fall into line agreeing with a 'yes' to the proposition as Karen remains quiet. The Chairperson repeats the question; does she feel the children are at risk? Karen is directed at least twice that she must agree for the benefit of the children and she can't abstain from the vote. The Chairperson informs her that everyone present must vote.

Karen struggles as she continues to state her reasons why she feels that our children are safe but the Chairperson talks above her, stating that there is no choice but to agree. I realise that the meeting is a travesty, designed to invoke a false sense of fair play. The vote was already agreed.

I look directly ahead as I speak only to Karen, "We need you, don't lose your job over this, you have no choice." Her eyes fill with emotion as she slowly nods, our GP following suit. Mark's name is added in the category of 'At Risk of Physical Harm' and Sean's in the category of 'Physical Harm' on the basis of one doctor's insistence and alleged possibility.

With confirmation that my children are now officially 'at risk' I rise from my seat in time to see Darron returning through the door. With a shake of my head I convey the outcome and he knows instantly what I mean, he understands that the meeting is over and walks back out of the door. I turn to face the entire assembly and, with tears streaming down my face, through massive sobs, as clearly as I can muster I raise my voice slightly as I state passionately: "You all know we'd never hurt our children, I hope you can sleep tonight!"

Darron and I walk back through the security doors but they have barely closed when I feel a hand grip my arm. "Can we have a word?" Mary Howard's hand steers me to one side, a man stands behind her and to the left. Ushered back in to the small side room we take a seat, defeated and despondent we no longer care what they say next, not at least until they say it.

The questions come thick and fast: "Have we mentioned everything?", "Have we forgotten something important like a fall down the stairs or a significant car crash?" The suggestions are preposterous. How can you forget anything like that? The propositions keep coming though, each one more ludicrous than the last as Mary continues "If you confess we can help you, we can get anger management training, we can give you support. Everything will go away if you just provide a reason."

Darron and I simply look at each other and shake our heads in utter disbelief. We had been with each other for most of Sean's life before he was taken ill. Sean and I had been in hospital, then staying at my Mum's and after that the midwife and health visitor had been visiting. There wasn't time to forget anything. Mary Howard leaned in closer, grasping her hands in her knees as she looked at me and said, "It would be better if you told us you know…better if you confessed."

Darron, on the verge of losing his temper all day, finally snapped and shouted: "Don't you think we'd remember a car crash? Do we look dim? How can we confess to something when we don't know what we are supposed to be confessing to?" I couldn't have put it better myself. We were being led. The suggestion was that if we admitted to abusing our son we could all go home like one little happy family. Like hell we could!

The children would be the subject of a court order in hours if we did that. We weren't falling in to the trap — we hadn't done anything. I looked her in the eyes and stated: "It is a charade. The meeting, the investigation, it is a witch hunt. We never injured Sean and we will never confess to something we never did." More pressure and threats follow as they state that the children can be removed immediately. I sense Darron tense and reach for his phone. In my heart of hearts I don't know what would have happened if they had tried to remove Mark and Sean.

My parents are waiting for us back at their house, but their willingness to protect their grandchildren would have come first. We had alluded to it before the meeting, all of us sensing that something wasn't right. Could we hide the children if the need arose? If we did, surely we would be assumed guilty by any court in the land, regardless of our innocence. There was no choice, we had to stand and fight and we had to win.

As Mary Howard and her line manager, Peter, continued to add pressure they would later record we 'failed to break'. We hadn't come this far to let our sons down. They however, still had the trump card. "We need you out of your house by 9.00p.m. tonight. The children and you need to be with someone twenty-four hours a day. You are no longer allowed to care for your children alone. We shall be in touch." I question the legality of the request and Mary Howard declares that *she* runs her cases and that "Legal don't tell me what to do".

Darron and I drive back to my parents' house as they are awaiting news of the meeting and both of us talk over the other in our rush to formulate a plan. Who can stay with us twenty-four hours a day? We all have jobs, mortgages and bills to pay. It is a little after 6.00p.m. and we have been given only three hours to go back to our home twenty minutes away, pack our bags and the children's things and find someone to care for all of us. We have been told that if we have not fulfilled the requirement by 9.00p.m. Mark and Sean will be taken into the care of the Local Authority.

We pull up on the drive and virtually run into the house, we cuddle the children and as fast as we can we bring my parents up to speed on where we stand. There are a lot of emotions and disbelief that in England today you can be made to leave house and home without any evidence of any wrong doing. Try as we might, we can't get over the fact that both of my parents work full time. Darron's family all live away and he still needs to get to work in the village where we live. Mark, who regularly attends playgroups, swimming and other social activities, would need to be able to carry on with as many of these activities as practically possible.

We leave the children with my parents, immediately getting in the car and driving home in shock at the speed of it all. As we rush home to pack, with no definitive plan, we decide that we will have to stay with my parents over-night so that we can have time to talk the options over. It is already 7.00p.m. and by the time we get home and back it will be 8.00p.m., which wouldn't factor in any time to pack. We run into the house and start to shout to each other, trying to co-ordinate our efforts and minimise time in order to prepare everything a family of four might need.

Anyone who has gone on holiday with a toddler or a baby will know how stressful it is and how many things you need. We had a two year old and a two month old baby. We had two sizes of nappies, high chairs, booster seats and cots, nobody else had any of that. Our children were the only children in the family, there were no others. Nobody we knew had a house set up for children. We would have to take whatever we needed, wherever we went.

We literally flung everything in to the car that night, there was no folding neatly and no checklist to check off. We had left our home to go to a meeting. Pots are on the side, clothes are in the washing machine and in the dryer, and the fridge and freezer are full of food. There is no time to organise it all, we simply wash up and turn off the heating. As we lock the door we are still too shocked to get upset. How can this happen in a modern society? How can we be forced to do this? Surely this isn't legal? There is no way I could answer any of the questions spinning round my head. All I knew was that my children would be removed if I did not comply. There was no time to think twice and no need to; if we wanted to keep our children we would have to obey.

Arriving back at my mum and dad's, mum already has tea on. We aren't sure what is going to happen next, just that we will be receiving a phone call and that we have to be with my parents or another relative by 9.00p.m. The children are still up but it doesn't matter. We are glad to see Mark playing and Sean, sleeping as ever, looking for all the world like an angel. I hug them both tightly and, as I tuck them in, Sean in a a deep-sided drawer and Mark in a single bed, I whisper to them both: "Mummy and daddy love you and nobody else is going to have you." Darron, kissing them both in turn, adds: "They'll get you over my dead body."

At 9.15p.m. the phone rings. Mary Howard speaks directly to my dad. My dad is really what you might call the traditional type. A mechanical engineer by trade, he works as an estates (site) manager for a large local hospital. He is the sort of dad who fixes things -cars, bikes, cookers, washing machines and vacuum cleaners. I laugh out loud as I write the last one as my mum spent years cheerfully telling my dad her hoover was broken, desperate for a nice shiny new one. In fact, mum had got the only tri-coloured hoover I have ever seen. There were more spare parts on that hoover than there are on a Lego set!

Dad answers the phone in a serious voice, his temper was short I could tell, but he gave nothing away on the phone. He keeps his cool as he constantly barrages Mary Howard with questions and picks fault with her answers. She tells him that she hasn't rung to speak to him; he replies she must have, since she was calling his house. The game was futile and clearly only serving to wind up our social worker, but for that very reason it was worth it and we were glad of the moral support.

Looking back, I am sure she was fed up with the mountain of paperwork she had probably had to wade through that day. She had tried to balance the risk of Sean being injured by us and she must have been out on quite a limb, bearing in mind he was still in our care. The lies and deceit, though, had done nothing to endear her to us.

Dad confirmed our presence and that of the children at their address, passing Darron the phone. Darron was informed that we would be visited again in the morning. Mary Howard reiterated that failure to stick to staying with relatives for twenty-four hours a day would result in immediate removal of the children. If we were not willing or were not able to comply with Social Service's requests, the children would be removed. Any deviation from the newly formed care plan would mean the removal of the children. In short, anything we did that hadn't been agreed first would result in our children being taken from their parents and placed in the care of the Local Authority.

CHAPTER 13.

We quickly realise that we need to be with someone who isn't at work and who can spend all their time with us. We need someone who won't mind being woken up in the night by a young baby and woken early in the morning by a small toddler. There was only one person we could think of.

My maternal grandma was retired and lived in a two bedroom bungalow. It wasn't ideal for a growing family, but she liked dogs and wouldn't mind having Mackie around and she obviously adored the children. We place a call at 9.30a.m. and ask her if she will take us all in. I feel awful even having to ask. She is a fit and active seventy-six year old but she is used to her own space and independence, it didn't seem fair.

Grandma agreed without hesitation, a note of defiance in her voice told me that she would do whatever it took, whatever was necessary. I came to appreciate later how steely she was. She certainly wasn't the frail great-grandma that Mary Howard or the local police were expecting, like the rest of the family she stood to lose a lot. Mark and Sean were her only great-grandchildren, the first children born to the family in nearly twenty-five years and the mere threat of them being taken into care sent her into a cold, determined fury.

My grandma isn't the kind of woman to scream and shout. She is level headed and intelligent, although her children, including my mum, would pull her leg at the last remark. Having been a company director and mother of three and now in her eighties she has plenty of life experience. For visit after visit Gran kept quiet. Speaking only when asked or interjecting only when she could take no more of the lies and falsehoods. From the outset, like the rest of our friends and family, she stood by us.

With my own mum working full time, when I had become a new mum it had been my grandma who had stepped into the breach when I was lonely or down. I would push Mark's pram up to her house in the evenings when he wouldn't stop screaming and when the rocking motion had sent him to sleep I would be glad to arrive at her immaculate bungalow for a cup of tea and a chat. I had never really seen her lose her temper. Even in all the years my brother and I had stayed at her house as children I had only ever encountered her 'stern voice'. She wasn't the type to yell loudly or the type to fuss, she was calm and capable and sometimes more than a little stubborn. I have never seen her over emotional as that just isn't her.

Widowed for over twenty years she has adjusted reluctantly to life on her own enjoying a variety of interests and travelling extensively. I, of course, know when she is angry, I know her very well, but to an outsider it is almost imperceptible. Many a time I would watch her as the social worker spoke, knowing what was in her mind I would wonder if they knew how close to the wire they were sailing. In all the time we stayed with her, she never once lost her temper, she always stated her point succinctly and with authority. The only word she would ever use in anger was 'poppycock!' and I respected her so much for that. Her calm manner often kept the situation from escalating and I knew that the burden we all carried was affecting her health but the alternative was unthinkable.

We decamp at my grandma's house on the 3rd March 2004. I unpack the bags and try to work out if we have everything we need. I call Peter, the line manager at Social Services, to advise him of our whereabouts and provide our new address. Darron is already back at work, having taken paternity leave and then additional leave whilst Sean was in hospital. Mary Howard takes to telling me often how much easier it must be having an extra pair of hands to help.

Actually I was capable of managing just fine without the need to wander about the Derbyshire Hills like some long-lost, nomadic tribe. I would have liked to visit my grandma's for social reasons, share a cuppa and a club biscuit and be normal. Somehow Mary never grasps that the restrictions are suffocating and impractical. Perhaps it is something to do with her never having had a child.

The following day, Mary phones in the morning to demand a meeting in order for us to sign an agreement for the twenty-four hours, seven days a week monitoring. When I ask her why there needs to be a written agreement I am subjected to more threats that the children can be removed and put in to care at any given moment. Mary Howard eventually makes the visit after a further two phone calls, both inferring the removal of the children should any hint of non-compliance be detected.

I take the opportunity to ask for minutes of the case conference, as I want to send them to our newly-appointed solicitor. Mary makes an excuse about the lack of minutes by regaling me with needless woes about her office printer. To be brutally frank I am not interested. The failure of an inanimate piece of hardware is the least of my worries, the irony of course being that I am a computer engineer.

The agreement, which has not suffered at the hands of the printer gremlin, has been put in front of me and I stall a little for time. I have no idea what half of the legal jargon refers to and I am tired and stressed. I still have to get up in the night to feed my baby, who is still recovering from a life threatening illness, and I still have to get up in the morning to a lively toddler who wants breakfast by 7.30a.m.

In a bid to gain some time to read the document I make reference to the fact that Darron is not present to sign it and defer the signing until the following day. I hope that first thing in the morning I will be able to contact the solicitor and ask her advice, but I am told that Social Services must keep the agreement. The page is put quickly back into Mary's bag and she alludes to the fact that the children can only remain with us if we sign it.

Gran, who has sat in virtual silence during the whole of this exchange, casually asks in a caustic tone, "It's strange you know, I worked for the Local Authority for many years before I retired and I have never known them to only have single copies of any agreements." Gran's comment hasn't gone unnoticed, as Mary turns ever so slightly to face her but fails to make further comment. Grandma continues her derision of the whole process as I watch Mary Howard get up and leave, walking down the drive before getting into her car. My mind is racing, what are we being asked to sign and for how long are we agreeing to it for?

The following day brings no more news and Mary Howard again arrives, still with only one copy of the agreement. Following a phone call earlier in the day from Mary, I have told her that we will need to seek legal advice on the contents of the agreement, but as she sits in my grandma's living room she puts increasing pressure on Darron and me to sign it there and then.

The threats come thick and fast, whilst we try to ascertain who has demanded this agreement. Apparently, Mary's line manager has instructed her to get the agreement signed and we take a gamble and refuse on the grounds that we have not been able to seek legal advice and the solicitor's office is now closed for the evening. It is a huge risk and we wonder what will happen next, but equally we have not been able to check the contents with our solicitor.

We are not being deliberately awkward, we are co-operating with everything we have been asked. We have no intention of breaking the twenty-four hour monitoring requested. However, we feel unable to trust what we are being told and therefore have no intention of signing anything without legal advice.

The weekend is a long one. We are expecting a serious fall out on Monday morning and only hope that we can get a message to our solicitor before Social Services get to us. The telephone has been ringing constantly, with Mary Howard placing calls about visits, paperwork and always adding the essential comments about the removal of the children into care. I am surprised when I manage to get to playgroup on Monday morning with both children, the phone having remained silent.

As always, I have to be in the presence of someone else and my friend Suzanne was great. Her endless support and willingness to listen to what must have been hours of rants at the injustice of it all, the tearful outbursts when everything got on top of me, and her patience in the times when I just struggled to raise a smile, made her the perfect companion. Suzanne was much more confident than me. Her son was only a few weeks older than Mark but she was older than I was and I admired her self assurance. Suzanne would always wade in if she felt a child was being bullied or intimidated and she didn't take any nonsense, she had firm ideas and yet she was caring and compassionate.

During the many times she accompanied me with the children to all sorts of outings she always tried to come up with new ways to help me out of the predicament I had landed in. Some suggestions were downright daft, others were hilarious, and occasionally she would hit upon a brilliant idea that hadn't occurred to Darron or me. In short she was invaluable.

Her car pulls up outside Gran's house on Monday 6th March. Jacob is already falling asleep and she is wiggling his foot with one hand that she now had tucked up behind her back. Car journeys always seemed to make Jacob drift off and he always seemed to want to sleep at dinnertime. Suzanne's continuous attempts to keep him awake in order to feed him were always met with a stubborn refusal as Jacob dozed on oblivious. I used to find this a source of endless amusement and if she was driving I would be tasked with keeping him awake.

Like most men I know, sleep is something they have down to an art form and it clearly starts young. I never succeeded in keeping him awake all the way home, sometimes I nearly made it to the drive, more often than not we had barely left the playgroup when he nodded off.

The day is fine and has a spring-like feel as I carry Sean in his car seat and cajole Mark up the long front path as his attention is diverted to the front lawn and the inclination to run around the mature trees that grow there. Grandma stands on the top step, it is unusual for her to meet me at the door and as I wave to Suzanne's car, already part way down the avenue, I intuitively ask "Is everything alright?" as she ushers me inside.

I can tell that something has happened. She pauses, trying to phrase it carefully, but the power of the words takes my breath away. "Heather love, the police have been here asking for you and Darron, they want to question both of you." I feel winded, as if someone has punched me in the chest. I want to ring Darron immediately, more for reassurance and support than for anything practical he can do. I wait, trying to compose myself, and decide it is better not to disturb him at work. My resolve weakens quickly as I think about what it means. They believe we have hurt our child, they think we have abused him.

I call immediately before having time to reconsider and the phone rings a number of times, unaware of the urgency. I am just about to hang up when his voice comes on the line, "Hello, what's up?" The question doesn't cover it, but he knows me too well. There is no way I would call him at work unless there is a problem. It is like the feeling you get when someone calls late at night or early in the morning and you automatically wonder who it can be and make the assumption that maybe something has gone wrong. This was no different, he knew at once that something had gone wrong as I simply whispered, "It's the police; they want to talk to us".

Later, it transpired that two police officers had knocked on my Grandma's door that morning asking to come in and wait for us. My Grandma had been the epitome of calm as she had informed them that we might be some time and they should perhaps call back. The more senior officer had gone on to explain the seriousness of the situation and tried to coerce Grandma into letting them inside. She knew that there was no reason for them to be in her house and with the number of visitors that were now calling, she told me later that she felt annoyed that they had tried to pressurise her into agreeing to yet another two strangers invading her space, without just cause.

When she tells me what has happened I feel grateful that she is the competent and capable person she is, she could have been easily shaken by the appearance of two police officers at her door and I have to admit that I would have certainly felt panic stricken. However, her husband, my grandad had been a serving police officer for a number of years and her uncle had been a chief superintendent in Manchester.

Police officers were just people to Gran and she took them as such, being polite but firm until they eventually agreed to call again later. The sergeant had thanked her for her time before telling her that, during their initial enquiries, nobody had a bad word to say about her granddaughter. She had merely replied: "No you wouldn't!"

The police, dressed in plain clothes, visit in the early afternoon and stay just long enough to give me a date and time for the interview. After they leave I start to make phone calls to our solicitor in a desperate attempt to obtain legal representation. Our solicitor, Julie was over forty minutes away in Hyde and as I call her office to speak with her I am told she is with another client. There is nothing I can do except to leave an urgent message for her to call me and sit and wait.

—

97

My grandma is already vocalising her thoughts on the matter through gritted teeth. These mainly constituted the words 'ridiculous' and 'pressure tactics'. I'm not really listening but the angry murmurs are an outward sign of support and I am glad she is there.

We wait a full half hour and as I pace up and down her long living room I think that surely they must know we would never hurt Sean or Mark. That is just it though, a few months ago I would have classed this whole situation as far fetched and unbelievable. Now we are under virtual house arrest, unable to go anywhere with our children and, although never formally accused, under suspicion. We are living a day by day existence. I'm not sure of anything anymore.

Grandma and I continue to wait for the sound of the phone ringing. At times the room falls silent, at times we chat about nothing in particular and then we discuss the release the previous year of Sally Clarke and Trupti Patel, wrongfully accused of murder. Was the witch hunt still continuing, would that soon be me? My gran makes a cup of tea in true British fashion and I stand looking out of her large picture window. From here, in the distance, you can see the Derbyshire hills, the spring flowers starting to bud and the world seems peaceful and quiet.

The peace is broken by the phone as it emits a high ringing sound. I have always found it funny how some people describe a phone urgently ringing, but whilst we are alert, fighting an invisible enemy, our senses are heightened. The shrill ring seems almost deafening as I run into the hall to pick up the phone.

"Julie?" I ask, barely waiting for an answer, "The police want to speak to us, we need a solicitor." Julie is a mother of two, blonde, tanned and a professional family lawyer who encourages me to remain calm. I barely know her really but she is the one who provides me with advice and I am looking to her for our next move. "It won't be me Heather, I only deal with family law. I will speak to my colleague Mr Wild, he deals with criminal law."

That phrase was like a spear. The word 'criminal' is all I hear as the conversation continues. I thank her as she hangs up, promising to try and arrange a solicitor and promising to call back and confirm. I suppose I have always known that if child abuse is suspected the police will obviously follow up the accusation and pursue lines of enquiry but it just doesn't seem real. I have never had so much as a ticket for littering and now my presence is 'requested' at the police station.

Darron comes home at the end of the day and without putting his bag down he comes to find out what has been happening. Our usual after work greeting of a kiss and a "How's your day been?" have long since been replaced with a resigned, hollow "Hello" and an expectant request for an update of news. I feel sick to the pit of my stomach, I'm not really eating and I have lost more weight. Every day I wake and for a few moments forget the nightmare, only to find it crashing over me in waves as soon as I am conscious enough to realise where I am.

In the middle of it all I am getting up several times every night to feed Sean and Grandma is having to do the same. I am supposed to be monitored at all times and this puts extra pressure on us all. I know that if I asked Gran would have been more than happy to do the night feeds on her own, but it has become a matter of principle and pride. I am Sean's mum and I am going to care for him. While I was on the earth and breathing he will never doubt that Darron and I love him and his brother and that we are his parents.

CHAPTER 14.

The next day passes with the usual round of repeated phone calls, visits and Mary Howard's continued insistence that we are lucky to have the children. I don't feel lucky, nothing feels less like luck than how I feel. I make a point of again asking Mary for the minutes of the case conference in order to read through them before the police interview.

As a person who has spent most of her life working with computers, and despite being dyslexic, I am always comforted by copious amount of paper. I feel reassured by writing things down, sometimes to the daft extreme of making lists just to cross things off them! I like to have a physical reference and I want to check that the conference minutes are accurate. Apparently though, they are still not available.

The Police interview takes place on Wednesday 10th March 2004. Any questions we have had about the police interview have been answered by Mary with a simple, "We don't have anything to do with the police side of things." Darron and I drive the fifteen minutes to the station repeating endlessly that the whole system seems unfair. We have been told by Julie that our solicitor today will be Mr. Wild and that he will meet us there.

We are anxious, upset and nervous. I have never even stepped foot inside a police station before and I have no idea what to expect as we walk through the large double doors. We are asked to take a seat in the foyer whilst the receptionist goes to find the officer who is conducting the interview.

Darron, forever a people watcher, tries to keep himself occupied by watching the car park and nudges me as a man in a black leather coat walks up the front steps.

He is over 30, with short dark hair, he is not tall but he exudes confidence. I watch him report to reception and hear the sound of my own surname as clear as glass. We rise from our seats as the receptionist points in our direction. "Mr Wright?" Darron ventures and he is greeted by a smile and a nod which is quickly followed by firm handshakes to both of us.

Mr Rob Wright is clearly much more at ease in his surroundings than we are. He strides about the foyer looking over the desk and beckoning the receptionist away from the photocopier. "I will need some time with my clients please, in private." I feel apprehensive, is he too confident? Is he giving the wrong impression? I have no idea what to do in these sorts of circumstances and Darron looks at me with a similar bewildered expression.

It seems only moments pass when Sergeant Hutton, accompanied by a female officer appears from the opposite side of the security doors and beckons our solicitor into a small room just off the entrance hall. Still completely perplexed I stare at the door for inspiration and a small clue as to what is going on behind it.

The meeting, if you could call it that, was brief to say the least. The two officers emerge and Rob gestures for us to join him. I try to read his expression but he gives nothing away. He asks me to sit down opposite and to go over the previous few months. I try to give as much detail as possible as I rake back over so much old ground.

The memories have become like a scab that is forever being picked off. The wound is still raw but the scars are already present. There is no time to heal the hurt because we are being dealt continual blows. I repeat and repeat, clarifying minor details as best as I can, hoping that the man before me can unravel the mystery better than I can. The time goes quickly and we have only been given a few minutes with our solicitor since meeting him and the interviews are due to start.

Rob checks his watch as he continues to ask questions and take notes before eventually sitting back in his chair and looking me straight in the eye and claiming: "To be perfectly frank, Heather, they have nothing, even in cases where they are sure it is hard to prove. All they have disclosed is that, in their view, even the queen can lose her temper and shake a baby but that isn't evidence and they know it. I was going to advise you to say 'no comment' throughout the interview but I have spoken to you and listened to your arguments for a medical cause. I think you just need to tell them exactly what you told me. You and I know you have nothing to hide and it's you they are going to try and pin this on because you are the primary carer. You need to try and remain composed and tell your side of the story." He pauses and turns slightly then continues "Darron, I presume you agree with the facts as Heather has just given them to me?"

Darron nods and starts to add more vehement denials of any wrong doing but is immediately stopped by Rob raising his hand. "Sorry but times short. Just tell them the truth and stick to the facts. If you don't know the answer, don't guess. They will try to trip you up and make you out to be liars. Stick to the facts. OK, come on."

We are led out of the room, through the security doors, out of the back of the building and into a much darker corridor. The side room we are shown into is no longer painted in a soft cream, with the bright lights of the public entrance, but a dark mustard yellow reminiscent of the mental health ward at the hospital. I immediately make the link to that other room with its black metal bars where the accusations first started.

The light is a fluorescent strip, dim and vaguely flickering, and I notice there are no windows. We are informed that we will be interviewed one at a time, the other one of us is to remain in the dingy cupboard-like room until called.

I am shown to a seat opposite Sergeant Hutton, his female colleague sits opposite Rob, our new solicitor. Rob's confident demeanour is reassuring but takes away none of the sickness and anxiety I feel having to answer questions in relation to abusing my own son. As the tape is loaded into the machine and the formality of a caution is observed I try to take in my surroundings.

The room is not as large as you see them portrayed on television, there would be no room for a camera crew in here. I realise that the door is behind the officers and I am in the corner, trapped between the table and the wall. I am now in the situation of a criminal, having already been informed that failure to meet with the police's request would have meant arrest. I have no choice but to be here and to answer their questions but as I read the paper on the table something begins to click in my brain.

For many years I have been able to see words in a different light, struggling to read as a child and left-handed initially, I learnt to write right-handed following a spate of bullying from another child. It has left me with the unusual ability to write with both hands. I am ambidextrous and my party trick is to write two words with both hands at the same time forwards, backwards and one forwards and backwards. It seems no different to me, but it always amuses others. In order to read, I struggled to comprehend letters but could easily see patterns in words this means that I can easily read upside down with no problem at all.

The sheets of A4 are placed flat on the table facing the Sergeant, whilst he fiddles with the tape player. I read as much as I can. The paper has been copied and is no longer level; the first line is cut so that now it reads: "To be questioned in response to an alleged unexplained." The word injury is missing and therefore it no makes no sense at all. I wonder if 'unexplaining' is now a crime and realise that ironically it is.

We have been told that it is the failure to explain a cause for the injury that is the problem. We have been told by the social worker that if we had concocted some story about how Sean was injured none of this would have happened. Somehow I doubt it.

I read on a few sentences more, the whole page written in bullet points and in a familiar style. The paper is lined with a margin and originally, before being copied, it had holes punched in. The familiarity eats away at me as I am drawn back to the present with the start of questioning. I repeat the history, my belief that there are many factors that could have meant Sean haemorrhaged. I state that it is not my place to diagnose an injury — that is the job of a medical professional.

I pull out vast amounts of paper from the file I have been carrying, producing the report of Dr. Timmin and, as I do so, the Sergeant refers to his copy of the report, which now I realise is stapled to an elusive copy of the case conference minutes. Rob looks edgy, this wasn't in the discussion and I think he is considering stopping me but waits momentarily to see what unfolds.

I turn the paper so that all four of us can see it and in as strong a voice as I can muster, state clearly: "It says here 'possibility of N.A.I.' are the courts in England now allowed to prosecute on possibilities? Are they allowed to jail parents for failure to diagnose their own children? Is it normal practice to arrest someone on the say-so of one doctor, who has no evidence and is merely offering an opinion?"

I look to Rob for support, his mouth upturns slightly at the corners but he says nothing and sits back in his chair, confident that I haven't talked myself into a cell.
The police officers look at me for a moment, perhaps they too have children, I see them change their tack as they push on, needing to fulfil their own jobs but a little less insistent.

Buoyed up by the minor and inconsequential victory I start to retaliate until finally they get to the final point on the list. 'Did mum shake Sean after he stopped breathing?' The officers go tit for tat as they question me endlessly; they start to suggest that it is understandable that a mum would shake her baby, particularly in response to the baby having stopping breathing. Surely, they allege, it would be natural to try and 'shake the baby awake?' Their ludicrous suggestion only serves to infuriate me.

It is now repeatedly suggested that I have shaken Sean when he had stopped breathing. Astounded at the concept, I see how easy it is to point the finger, I had bathed him alone, I had called Darron only after he had seemed to stop breathing, I had no alibi.

How many people bath a child in pairs I wonder? How many people think they need a witness to the fact their child has stopped breathing? I realise that the accusation could never be defended. The time of the alleged injury was not defined, in fact we had been given differing opinions on what the injury consisted of. Birth was given as the time of part of the injury, but another doctor gave further injury time indicating abuse.

I was weary, sleep deprived and fed up of fighting an accusation that I couldn't disprove. Angrily I denied it until the repetition became like machine gun fire and I countered: "As far as I know, shaking is not a recognised form of resuscitation!" The questioning stopped for a split second and the volume level that had been creeping up lowered as Sergeant Hutton posed his final question "Did you shake Sean?"

With tears falling on to the plain grey table I shook my head. The sergeant gave me a sympathetic look and spoke in a milder tone, "For the tape, we need it for the tape." With the defiance of a parent who knows their own innocence I tried to convey it all in a single and determined "No!"

I leave the room so that Darron can take his turn. Rob has advised me that I had done the right thing in speaking. I had not hidden behind a defence of 'no comment', I had gone on tape refuting everything they had offered as possible motive and so called evidence.

Darron's interview takes a fraction of the length mine had taken. They can obviously offer no reason or particular opportunity for Darron to have committed the alleged offence. In actual fact a year later another doctor would make out Darron was the new prime suspect; there would be no new evidence, just another suggested possibility of the likely culprit.

As we stand on the steps to the police station we shake hands with Rob Wright for the last time and he smiles again readily. "You'll be fine, that was just a fishing exercise. Try not to worry." It's much too late for that though, it has been months since worry was the only feeling I felt upon waking and the last feeling before falling, if possible, into an exhausted and fitful sleep.

The drive back to my grandma's is easy, it is a working day and the roads are quiet. Darron and I continue one of the many circular conversations that go round in our heads constantly. Arriving back, we come through the door and the phone is already ringing, Grandma answers the call and her face clouds over. I can tell who it is before she passes me the telephone; the look she is giving me is one of pure contempt and it is reserved only for the social worker, Mary Howard.

Mary asks if the police are taking things any further but I don't know the answer any better than she does. It is in speaking to her that that I realise why the handwriting on the page at the police station was familiar. It was Mary Howard's handwriting.

In a call-log that I later obtain under the Freedom of Information Act I find a page of Mary's call-log where she records how she 'liaised' with the police about the interviews that were to take place. In the entire time she worked with us, Mary would maintain that the police were a separate entity and their investigation was not linked with her own. She would in short, lie.

The following day the newly formed 'core group' meets. It is a meeting of professionals and our family. Both of my parents have taken time off work to attend and Grandma is also present. Darron, Mark and Sean are all there with me as the meeting starts. We have talked to Karen and Gina frequently during the previous few days and they are aware of the strain we are under and we know that nobody in the core group had a say in the twenty-four hour monitoring.

Darron and I again ask for minutes of the case conference but Mary Howard replies that she doesn't have her copy. Yet again, copies of paperwork are scarce or missing and information is only recorded verbally, making it difficult to call anyone to account and allowing the social worker to back track or change stipulations at will.

Mary informs everyone present that all the core group can do is undertake a core assessment, as she passes around a singe copy for everyone to look at. I look briefly at the document and question why it has taken so long to start the assessment that is supposed to be completed by law in thirty-five days. Mary advises me that in actual fact the thirty-five day deadline is flexible. Darron adds that, in this case, it seems to be the only thing that is.

Mary Howard threatens on two occasions during the meeting that failure to comply with any request made by Social Services will result in both of our children being taken into care. The meeting makes no real headway and, as it draw to a close and is finally declared over, I state my intention to call the Chairperson of the case conference to find out why our copy of the minutes have not been sent.

Within half an hour of her leaving, Mary Howard telephones us to say that our copy of the minutes is on her desk and that she will post them to us. Darron and I exchange knowing glances, we both know their arrival is more than a little coincidental. In actual fact, when the minutes arrive several days later they are missing a number of reports, including the initial report made by Dr. Fieldman.

That initial report has not been given to anyone at the conference; only the report by Dr. Timmin is included. It seems that in family courts you can cherry pick the 'evidence'. It appears to us that in Britain in 2004 you can have your lives turned upside down by one line, written by a doctor in one report and taken as the truth by a system that allows possibility to be taken as fact. The argument is cyclic—the doctor suggests possible abuse and expects Social Services to investigate; Social Services investigate and conclude abuse based on the doctor's possibility.

There was no medical expert to testify to any contributory factors. The cause had been given by Dr. Andrew Timmin over the phone and recorded in the Social Services call-log as 'indicative of a circular motion such as a shake.' He had gone on to state that a child could fall between four and six feet without a skull fracture. This wasn't relevant since we weren't discussing anyone with a skull fracture, but the inference was clear. In order to sustain such 'traumatic' injuries as those that Sean was said to have sustained, you would need to use extreme violence.

CHAPTER 15.

By Friday 12th March, Mary Howard has started the pattern that we would eventually come to refer to as 'The Friday Bombshell'. This tactic normally involves making our visit the last call of the day on a Friday, following a string of sometimes irrelevant phone calls, which never fail to mention the possibility of our children being removed.

Mary Howard claims that following discussions, it has been decided that the need for twenty-four hour monitoring needs to be changed so that my parents can care for the children, and a childminder is to care for them whilst my parents are not present. Mary Howard also tells us that the childminder will be expected to take notes whenever they are present, effectively giving access to our lives from 8.00a.m. until 5.50p.m, in addition to the visits already scheduled. We are again threatened that, although the arrangement is voluntary, failure to comply will result in the children being forcibly removed.

I make a frantic call to Darron, who is on shift for the evening, and within minutes he is on his way home, but Mary Howard chooses to leave before clarifying the situation. It is now too late to contact our solicitor or the line manager at Social Services. The bomb had been successful delivered and the weekend was a restless one.

The minutes of the core group meeting are received the following morning but they are frequently factually incorrect. My mum, who in addition to her work as a school bursar also acts as a Clerk to the Governing body, regularly takes minutes and she has set herself the task of minuting every meeting she attends. Her minutes record what the Social Services record does not. They note that conditions on our family had been imposed on the 2nd March, under threat of the children being removed, and that the core assessment should therefore run from this date.

The Social Services record states that the core group formulated a child protection plan. In actual fact the formulation was simply Mary Howard informing all those present of what they were expected to do, stating that if it was not done Mark and Sean would be taken into care. The record Mary Howard has provided refers to all agreements being voluntary but in fact they were all imposed by threatening the children's removal.

In fact, during the whole meeting, no staff member from Social Services picked up a pen, no Chairperson was appointed and no agenda was tabled. The meeting, like everything else we had come to witness, was farcical.

As Monday begins, the first visit is already underway at 9.00a.m. by Gina, the nursery nurse. Her happy smile and willingness to play eternally endeared her to Mark, who came to relish her visits and the toys she would bring to amuse him. Gina had barely finished her cup of coffee when the phone rings for the first time that day. I pick it up expecting to hear Mary, but instead it is Darron on the line.

Despite knowing our schedule inside and out, Mary Howard has called Darron at work to tell him that he must arrange time off to meet with her urgently. I hang up the phone and call the Social Services desk immediately. My temper is rising as I wonder what else she has concocted now. Why is she harassing us in this way?

After being on hold for a considerable length of time, Mary answers my call. Her voice is tentative and I can hear there is more to what I am being told that she lets on. We have been stressed all weekend following her demands on Friday and she didn't have the decency to wait for Darron then. I interrupt her and make a demand of my own, I want to know what is going on and I won't wait all day for her to visit later when she can tell me over the phone.

Mary Howard insists that the children will be taken into foster care immediately if we can't arrange for someone to care for the children twenty-four hours a day. We are no longer to provide any form of care to our children, someone else must do it and, as my Grandma is considered too old, we should ask my parents. If we do not or cannot comply, the Local Authority will take custody of Mark and Sean by the end of the day.

Shocked by yet another sudden change in direction, I advise Mary that both my parents work full time. She offhandedly replies that one of them should take time off for compassionate reasons and that if they did they would be eligible for a proportion of their salary. Still numb with disbelief I call Darron and ask him to come home immediately so that we can try to ascertain what we should do next. My mum and dad are both at work and, having repeatedly received similar threats, I am reluctant to phone them until I know for sure what is going to happen.

Darron arrives home and, as we discuss all the possible outcomes and ways around the situation, I express concern that yet again the course of action has changed without any more evidence or incidents. In fact, to the contrary, our parental assessment shows glowing reports of our children's abilities and of our parental skills. There have been no incidents and we have not stopped co-operating with Social Services. Darron calls Mary's line manager in order to find out why there is a sudden change in the plans.

I only hear one side of the call, listening only a few feet away as Darron first waits on hold to speak to Peter, Mary's line manager, and then his initial introduction before launching into a direct request for reasons as to why we are no longer capable of parenting our children. I hear Darron's voice rise as he says, "In my line of work if a line manager claimed not to know what his staff were doing he would be sacked."

I come to the conclusion that Peter claims to be unaware of the request for alternative care of the children.

Darron speaks with his hand over the receiver as he tells me that he is being transferred back to Mary in order to ascertain more. In the end, after several phone calls we are told that we must find someone to take over daily care of Mark and Sean or they will be removed forthwith. We are no further forward in establishing why this change is required and as Mary informs us she needs to visit to discuss the matter, we refuse. We have already had one visit that day and at least six phone calls and we need time to regroup.

Throughout the whole of the time Mary Howard is assigned as our social worker it seems that pressure tactics are key to making us comply. Any requests are always at the last minute and only ever directed at one of us. We are constantly bombarded and we are given no time to consider our options. The next day this proves to be the case again as Mary calls to speak to Darron about what plans he has made for the care of the children, but he is working and can't hear the phone.

In total, she calls Darron three times, knowing he is at work; she calls our house phone several times, knowing us to be living elsewhere; she calls my parents home phone twice before eventually calling my grandma's house. Due to the messages she leaves, we work out that all the calls take place within four minutes. She leaves a final message on Darron's mobile to call her.

Eventually Mary Howard arranges to visit us at my grandma's house as she has done on so many previous occasions. Had she phoned me there initially I could have taken the call, but for some reason she did not. After her arrival she reiterates that my parents have been chosen to care for the children, with no thought of asking them directly.

Grandma is considered too old and so Mary maintains that my mum and dad are the best carers for Mark and Sean and they will have to 'make arrangements.'

We inform her that our solicitors have been in touch with Social Services legal team and that no such specification has been made. It seems that, yet again, the decisions that were being made had no correlation to procedures or what had been decided in the meetings with the other professionals.

Darron and I are exhausted with trying to fight a system that seems determined to break us for no other reason than the fact that we haven't confessed to something we haven't done. Up until the police interview the whole issue of the injury caused had been glossed over with the all encompassing non-accidental injury phrase. I was now spending vast amounts of time trying to find alternative causes for subdural haematomas and I was gradually building up a picture of something that had no firm basis in fact.

The concept of 'shaken baby syndrome' had first been introduced by Dr. John Caffey in 1946, and it was initially referred to as "whiplash shaken infant syndrome". Dr. Caffey was a paediatric radiologist, who was trying to hypothesise that a number of specific symptoms found with little or no external evidence of head trauma, including retinal hemorrhages and intracranial hemorrhages in addition to bone fractures, could be caused by a shaking mechanism. One of the articles he wrote on the matter states that, in his opinion, the number of such whiplash shaken baby cases is incalculable but substantial.

Today's literature is divided between those who firmly believe in Shaken Baby Syndrome and those who question the validity of an unproven diagnosis. Those supporting such a label claim that even children who may appear symptom free go on to have learning disabilities or global developmental delays once they start school.

Spontaneous bruising and bleeding are a feature of other disorders, which should be checked by a haematologist. Genetics, birth trauma, accidental injury and other factors can also give rise to similar scan findings but correct medical diagnosis is not pursued once the blame has been laid firmly at the parents' door.

By the 19th March, another Friday, we have endured a week of constant telephone calls from the Social Services offices and repeated and reiterated threats about the removal of the children. All of this culminates in Mary Howard knocking on the door of my grandma's house shortly after 10.00a.m. She has already made two calls since starting work that morning and she demands that Darron and I are present as she needs to interview us individually.

In my view, looking back on the case records it appears that the police have advised her there is no case to answer and, in desperation, she is interviewing us herself in the hope of getting something the police did not. In short she is hoping for a full confession.

Darron is to be interviewed first and, after a brief discussion, Mary Howard lays out her papers on my gran's dining table telling Grandma and myself that we will have to keep out of the way during the interview. I observe that in a two bedroom bungalow with one living room and a kitchen diner she has now effectively banned us from getting any drinks or snacks. Bearing in mind that we have a small baby and a toddler in the house, I consider if she has ever thought about the practicality of her suggestion, but based on past form I quickly conclude that she probably hasn't. In fact the 'interviews' go on until a quarter to two, nearly four hours after they began.

I obviously can't comment on the content of Darron's so-called interview, but I find the whole experience surreal. Mary repeatedly asks for an explanation of Sean's injuries whilst continually suggesting ridiculous scenarios and insinuating that any explanation would mean that the case would not have to go to court. I state unequivocally that I am not prepared to speculate on possible causes and I am told that a failure to 'come up' with an explanation will mean that I will lose my children.

In a rare offer of help Mary Howard mentions that she will look for an NNEB accredited nanny to provide the twenty-four hour monitoring required, but hours later she telephones withdrawing the offer as Derbyshire understandably has no funding.

As Mary walks down the front path again, I watch her leave and turn to my grandma who is rocking Sean gently in her arms. I gaze down at the baby who is not yet three months old and I can't help but think about what the future holds. My eldest son, barely two, plays with a jigsaw unaware of the battle we are fighting to keep him. Mark knows his family, knows his mum and dad and his surroundings, Sean is blissfully unaware.

My mind allows me to consider the possibility of a life without them, but the thought is fleeting, it is inconceivable, I will give everything I have in order to ensure their wellbeing and to me that means a childhood out of the care system. The conversation between the adults is strained and inconsequential; we are simply passing the time as another visitor is due. Fifteen minutes after the social worker leaves the family support worker, Caroline, arrives to continue the parental assessment.

It is 2.00p.m. and the day already feels long, none of us sleeps well anymore and we have all been up with Sean, who is a real lark. When the assessment finishes at just before four, Caroline gives us lots of praise for our parenting skills and handling of the children. I feel like I am taking part in some strange reality show, the comments are meant in an encouraging way but seem condescending. Mark has always been a happy child with lots of opportunities but Sean's life will be different.

The continual visits and the constant disruption make it hard to go anywhere without watching the clock endlessly. I no longer walk the dog for miles over the fields as Grandma would have to come too. I no longer walk to the shops for an idle look around because I know someone will have to accompany me. I can't even take my children to the park without a chaperone. I have no freedom and I have no say.

In a desperate attempt to feel useful and to help our situation I write a letter to our solicitor telling her of the harassment we are experiencing and the dramatic increase in visits and telephone calls of late. I ask her to clarify our situation, as we are no nearer to returning home and all the child safety measures we have put in place at our family home are now having to be put in place at my grandma's house and the home of my parents.

After a very emotional phone call, Julie tells me that the best thing is to enter into proceedings in order to force Social Services hand. Darron and I talk about it: surely Social Services take parents to court, not the other way around? On the advice of our solicitor we agree to demand a resolution to the situation and give them seven days to issue proceedings. The gauntlet is thrown down on the 17th March 2004.

CHAPTER 16.

The week that follows is a re-run of the previous weeks. Visitors come more than once a day, the phone rings endlessly and Mark is constantly asking who is who. He now thinks that Mary Howard is a member of the family and whenever we go home to pick up some more things, or even just to collect the post, he clings to the doorframe of the house crying 'Mark's house' over and over in a non-stop bid to stay.

We have called our home 'Mark's house' in the vain hope that he will remember where he lives. His room has been recently decorated with Bob the Builder pictures and a very large digger mural that I had painted on the wall. It is his new bedroom, a bedroom suitable for a 'big boy', now that the Tigger nursery with its mobiles and glow in the dark stars is needed for his little brother.

I had been so determined to finish Mark's room on time that I had stayed up until 4.00a.m. to paint it one night; unable to sleep because of the constant itching I was glad of a distraction. The room is now unused, I have already taken the bedding and washed it all ready for our return, but the house feels soulless without people living in it. We now pay increased insurance as the house is technically classed as vacant and we have had to ask a neighbour to keep watch on it for us. We have no idea how long we will be away from home and we live each day as it comes.

Each time we collect the post we check the phone for messages and a number of them are always from Mary Howard. I feel guilty that we haven't returned the numerous calls and messages from friends; some would later remark that when they hadn't heard from us they thought we were getting divorced.

Our lives are so busy with two small children and the repeated visits, appointments, calls and meetings that we feel too tired to phone everyone, even if we didn't feel guilty for using Gran's phone, it would be impossible for us to relay the changes that are taking place almost daily.

Grandma is doing a great job in looking after us all but, although we buy our own food and try to contribute, the loss of money from Darron's pay, due to the time off and the end of my maternity pay, means that financially we are losing ground. This only serves to add to the increasing stress we are under but it never seems to prevent the last minute requests for our attendance at meetings and visits, regardless of the fact we are trying to earn a living and bring up two children under three.

During March we take the decision to spend each weekend with my mum and dad as neither of them work weekends. This means that Grandma can at least find a small amount of time to have her house to herself and we can all get a break from each other. The only problem is that it also means the weekly packing and unpacking of all our things.

My mum and dad's house is huge, an old Victorian house with as many bedrooms as it has draughts. We had helped them move into it the February before our wedding and they had kindly put us up in between house moves. The large size is great for Mark to play football up and down the hallway, but the terrible state of repair means that dad, who is doing the repair work himself, has to stop working whilst we are staying. The increased space is a welcome change from the bungalow but we miss the cosy warmth and the nicely decorated surroundings. Mum and dad's house is a definite work in progress and with us staying there is much more work than progress!

The end of the month brings another core group meeting. This is mainly another exercise in the flexing of

Social Services' muscles. The meeting takes place, as the previous ones had, at our own home. The decision to use our house was made by the social worker before we had been asked to leave and the meetings had continued to be held there even though we were no longer living at the address.

We return for the meeting in time to make tea and coffee, endeavoring to offer refreshments, having had to bring milk with us. After the meeting I wash up and dry up before locking the door again. The whole situation feels like a farce, as there is nobody in the house for weeks and then the drive is full of cars and the house full of people for an hour or so, only for the emptiness to return minutes after the meeting has ended.

Mary Howard breaks the habit of the previous weeks and decides to drop her bombshell on a Thursday, as she informs us that Social Services will be going to court for an 'Interim Care Order'. I ask her why an order is necessary when we have co-operated with Social Services requests and she puzzlingly answers, "Just in case."

It is eight days since our demand for proceedings and we have an answer: Social Services want to obtain temporary parental responsibility whilst investigations continue. Darron merely replies; "Over my dead body!" I have no doubt in my mind that he means it.

The court hearing is heard at Chesterfield Magistrates court and we intend to do everything in our power to keep full parental responsibility for both children. It is inside the court building that we finally meet the barrister who has been instructed on our behalf. Kate is a mature woman with straight blonde hair in a smooth long bob. She looks every part the consummate professional and, as she shakes our hands firmly, she gets straight down to the point.

She bombards us with questions about what has been happening and declares that there is no need for an order to be made with full co-operation from ourselves already having been proven. She gives us confidence as she reads through the paperwork, pulling apart the inconsistencies and inadequacies of the Local Authority's argument.

The next hour is spent with her and our solicitor trailing back and forth between the two rooms, one with us in it and one with Mary Howard and the Derbyshire County Council lawyer. The magistrates are ready for us and yet the solicitors in the corridor outside the door are still in hasty animated discussions. We are shown through to a room where there is a very large square table and barely enough room around the edge for the chairs. We take our seats at one side with the Local Authority's representatives, including the social worker, on the other as our barrister and solicitor return.

Kate looks over to us and winks at us as the magistrates file in and we simply sit throughout the whole proceedings agreeing to continue to 'work with' the Local Authority before realising that no interim care order has been applied for. The magistrates talk to all of us advising us of the need to transfer the case to a higher court due to the medical complexities of the case. Darron and I nod in agreement but all we care about is that we will be going home tonight as the only people responsible for the care of our children.

The magistrates file out and the solicitors shake each other's hands as if they have been playing a friendly football match. Mary Howard comes over and wishes us well, adding that she is pleased no order has been requested or granted, contrary to everything she said at the core group meeting only days before. I smile half heartedly out of a sense of politeness, but Darron, not impressed by the pretence at solidarity, walks behind me to speak to our solicitor to find out what happens next.

We have already been advised that, due to our complaints about the number of threats to our children and the constant harassment, we have been assigned a new social worker. I know it is probably the last time I will see Mary again but I don't feel sad.

In a total of thirty-four working days in which she was connected with our case she made nineteen formal visits totaling twenty-six hours, forty-eight answered phone calls (not including messages) repeated interviews and demands to think up an explanation, and we were informed over fifty-six times that our children would be taken away from the family and put into care. This does not include the visits requested by Social Services from their own family support workers, the health visitor and the nursery nurse and unofficial visits from the social worker 'on her way home' or in order to leave paperwork,

I don't think there is any doubt as to the pressure, intimidation and bullying tactics employed in order to get us to admit abusing our son. I put it to Mary that Social Services involvement had not been constructive and that they had tried their best to destroy our family, she makes eye contact for the first time that day as she tells me that, if put under enough pressure, most parents will 'break and confess'.

In a court of law, a 'forced confession' is defined as a confession obtained by a suspect under torture or duress leading to the person being interrogated agreeing to the story presented to them or even falsifying facts in order to satisfy the interrogator and discontinue the suffering. A confession made by a person under threat or enticement is not admissible in evidence in UK law but it seems that this is not the case in family courts, where secrecy and hidden agendas lurk around every corner.

In fact, this issue and others like it were eventually to lead to a Family Justice Review as over two-hundred MP's called for an abolition of the secrecy surrounding family courts. We are still gagged by the system though. It is 2004 and reforms won't start for a further two years; we are trapped and silenced as we are told that we can't have any other family members present at court and we are not to discuss the case or our lives with anybody. We leave the court in Chesterfield having won the battle but with the war still raging.

It is Easter time and the start of spring in earnest and as we drive home we feel hopeful. Our case is to be passed to the County Court at Derby, as the evidence is complex and the case is not straightforward, but that will take time and for now we just have to comfort ourselves that our children are just that – ours.

As we arrive though the door of my parents' house, hugs are abound as we all celebrate the fact that we have achieved our goal of preventing a court order and we flop on the sofa feeling tired because of the sleepless nights and worry we have been experiencing. Nothing, though, detracts from the happiness we feel that the three magistrates agreed to let us keep our children and I relish reading them bedtime stories until way past bedtime.

CHAPTER 17.

The Easter holidays bring a new beginning in our day to day life as the new social worker starts to work with us. Marie shares a similar name to our previous social worker but here the similarity ends. She looks slightly older than Mary Howard but by her manner she demonstrates far more life experience and worldliness. The first time I meet her she talks briefly before getting on the floor and playing a game with Mark.

I am instantly put at ease as unlike her predecessor this social worker is only interested in the welfare of the children. I resolve to prove to her that we share the same goal. Her voice is calming and quiet and she is not at all confrontational. Marie listens as I tell her my feelings about the case and the frustration the whole family feels that the medical profession seemed to cast aspersions and then left us out in the cold, failing to follow up on any possible medical cause other than the one they had created.

Marie is not a blind believer or an unwavering accuser and I get the feeling that she will make her own mind up about the probable cause of Sean's injuries. She makes it patently clear that despite the court hearings and solicitors arguments we will have to work together and make the best of it. In spite of my willingness and need to dislike her, my respect grows as I understand that she must do her job and as a mother, I must do mine.

On the 19th April we travel to Derby County court as proceedings continue. The court is over an hour from our house and we leave exceedingly early to make sure we are on time. It is early days and we are not sure what to expect as we eventually file into the courtroom to listen to the judge's directions. We are fearful of what lies ahead and everything is out of our control, Darron and I cling to each other for support as the hearing begins.

It is a matter of minutes before the judge decides that the case must be transferred higher, to Manchester High court, due to the complexity of the evidence. We walk out having spent a sleepless night and anxious morning to no avail; we are no further forward. The next day, Tuesday, the case will be heard in Manchester.

Weariness dogs our every waking moment these days and the journey home is tiring, more from the lack of sleep than anything else. I wonder what the hearing in Manchester will bring and another restless night is a likely consequence. We decide to take the train to Manchester the following day as we have never driven into the city and are concerned about getting lost. The cost of the endless court hearings, days off work for meetings and travel expense is mounting and there is no end in sight.

Tuesday dawns early as we awake before it gets light. As we board the train, my nervousness is matched only by Darron's, neither of us knows what will happen or what we can do to get ourselves free of the situation we have been landed in. As we reach the court the doors are manned by security staff using metal detectors to check people for concealed weapons and who frisk you as soon as you enter the building. The court is modern in looks with traditional wood panelling inside, and there are lots of people all gathered into small groups. Wigged barristers gather together, sometimes calling to colleagues as they pass and sometimes hurrying along with suitcases containing case details.

It isn't long before Sean's case merits its own wheeled suitcase and I find this almost amusing as people in suits trundle them along, occasionally getting the absurdly small wheels stuck in the lifts or banging them into the rotund metal bins that seem set to booby-trap every corridor. The latter often causes a clang that makes everyone look round, which in turn causes the culprit to adopt either a nonchalant stare or an embarrassed look, depending on their status.

Our solicitor and barrister sit with us while we wait, occasionally crossing the hallway to speak to other solicitors that they are working with on other cases. Once you are in the system it soon becomes obvious that solicitors and barristers that specialise in family law can be instructed by the parents, the Local Authority or the Children's Guardian (the Guardian being a court appointed representative who speaks on behalf of the child or children). This leads to the solicitor or barrister you have instructed often having coffee and a chat with the Local Authority solicitor and barrister who are against you in court. Despite the client confidentiality clauses there is nothing more disturbing than seeing the solicitor on your case laughing out loud with the person you are fighting against in five minutes time.

The Judge who sits in Manchester that day is keen to find out why there are so many discrepancies in our case. Even the report of Dr. Timmin sometimes seems to contradict itself and the Local Authority denies having ever obtained it. This leads to a situation where Social Services claim to have acted on a report written by a doctor who had never seen Sean or had his medical notes. The judge asks the Local Authority if they are bringing care proceedings based on the report, but they deny any involvement with it.

It seems that although we have had to leave home and face the possibility of having our children removed from us, the report, that was used as the only indicator of abuse, is now being buried. I consider the prospect that maybe the way in which the report had been requested wasn't legal, is that why they are distancing themselves from it?

If Dr. Timmin had never written the report there would have been no grounds for Social Services to get involved with our family, yet prior to their involvement and afterwards we had retained parental responsibility. That meant that if someone had wanted to conduct tests our permission had to be sought; if a second opinion was needed we should have been asked. At no time were we informed that Sean's scans were being forwarded to another hospital and once the accusations had been made we are no longer allowed access to Sean's medical files in order to check for inaccuracies we knew existed.

Social Services were now claiming to have had no say in the instruction of Dr. Timmin, yet there were five documents on file, including a note made by Mary Howard asking Dr. Williams to obtain another opinion of Sean's brain scan, together with subsequent letters Mary had received from him. Why, if he was not connected to the Local Authority or Sean, had Dr. Timmin been asked his opinion with regard to different medical aspects of the case?

Social Services had brought care proceedings based on a single line in Dr. Timmin's report and yet now failed to acknowledge the report as evidence. Surely in a criminal court of law the case would have been thrown out? This isn't a criminal case though and the burden of proof is not 'without reasonable doubt' but on 'the balance of probability'.

In an alleged diagnosis of Shaken Baby Syndrome, and I use the word alleged diagnosis because the term refers to the mechanism of the injury and not actually the injury itself (which may consist of a subdural haematoma, retinal haemorrhages and/or swelling of the brain) the accusation is not defendable. Unless you have never spent any time alone with your baby you can never argue that you didn't have the opportunity, and no motive is required as all new parents are potentially stressed and sleep deprived.

Cases of shaking became more common for prosecution experts who couldn't explain the medical findings

126

scientifically and used the term to account for cases where initially the three symptoms were found, until gradually this altered so that only a subdural bleed was enough.

When a prominent British neuropathologist, re-examined the criteria she had used as a prosecution expert and realised it was flawed, she became the target of vicious personal and professional attacks. Her fellow professionals, who had made careers on the back of such findings, claimed she was the only one who held the belief that the science behind shaking injuries was flawed. The neuropathologist refuted the accusation in a number of newspaper and magazine articles. She stated that the opinion of other professionals in her field of expertise was not sought and that the mainstay of medical opinion is still just that, an opinion based on the view of neuroradiologists.

She and an increasing number of other pathologists state that scan findings by radiologists are not matched by post-mortem findings in infants, whose deaths have been attributed to shaking. Interpretations of images, whilst informative and useful, are still open to *mis*-interpretation and neuroradiologists continue to place parents and carers in the dock, repeating the same opinion every time they see a subdural bleed in an infant, whose carers had been left 'holding the baby' without a witness.

Meanwhile new opinions, formed following the study of the extensive research by another British neuropathologist, have been opposed by the Metropolitan Police, who are presumably worried about the number of cases that would have to re-opened if the cause of such injuries was found to be not abusive.

An increasing number of doctors are warning that a significant proportion of parents and carers could have been wrongfully convicted and that does not include those tried in secret in the family courts. In a family court the judge must be satisfied that on the 'balance of probability', the injury is *more likely* than not to have been abusive and that the perpetrator is the *most likely* to have committed the alleged act.

Social Services' offers of help are much more forthcoming by the end of April. Marie tries to offer practical help to us as a family, helping with sleeping arrangements and trying to ease the burden that the impositions have created. Her visits are cordial and at times there is even a little humour as Sean, now four months tries to grab anything to hand (or foot) and demand attention, sometimes sitting briefly before sliding over sideways.

The phenobarbitone Sean had been prescribed has caused a sedentary effect, which isn't apparent initially, as Sean is a quiet baby with only a few people ever seeing him awake. It isn't until the medication is reduced and finally stopped that Sean's true character emerges. Sean is no longer the quiet baby in the corner, he is an engaging baby, a baby who kicks his feet madly and waves his arms if anyone comes near him. He relishes attention and has started to love the introduction of solid food, making a fuss if anyone else is eating!

By early May, Sean can happily feed himself a rusk, roll over and over and pick up items with his feet and pass them to his hands. Despite the prognosis given by the doctors, he is developing normally. Mark continually encourages his little brother to try out new things and he watches over Sean protectively.

It is around this time we first come to meet the Children's Guardian, a person appointed by the court to act for the welfare of the child during court proceedings. The actions of the Guardian are influenced by their belief in what they feel to be the best interests of the child. A representative of the thoughts and feelings of the child themselves in a case of older children and for small infants someone who considers which outcome is best, based on informed and impartial judgment.

We recognise that the Guardian can make recommendations to the judge and these recommendations are possibly more influential than those of the social worker. If the Guardian wanted what was best for our children, surely they would share the same outlook as us, after all that is what we wanted too.

Isaac Bateman visits us at my parent's home on the 22nd April. He is not particularly tall, dark haired and appears approachable and friendly. I'm surprised that he spends such little time with the children, almost seeming uncomfortable in their presence. Perhaps this is because he is trying to remain objective, trying not to be distracted by Mark, who has brought him every toy in the near vicinity, and Sean, whose high pitched noises are matched only by the dog, whining to be let through the door to meet our newest guest.

He greets us with a firm handshake and accepts the offer of a drink, not least of all because he has travelled some distance to meet us. I had seen him briefly at the magistrate's court but I was unsure as to his role. He now explains fully to both of us, what he does and why he is here, pausing to sip his drink and smiling as he picks out a chocolate biscuit. For our part we listen attentively and hope that the winning mannerisms of our gorgeous sons are enough for him to see that we are a family and that we need to stay together.

Isaac points out the holes in Social Services' arguments but remains professional as we ask him questions he is unable to answer, referring us instead to our solicitor. I have held the belief for a while now that knowledge is power and the more I can learn the better. I am hoping to pre-empt every move and find some way of getting our children back home, and I am not ashamed to push my luck on occasion by prying a little further than is strictly acceptable. Whenever I do, I am greeted by a small hint of a smile and downcast eyes, leading me to apologise to Isaac for the awkwardness of the request, but in truth I don't really mean it—I will go as far as I am allowed leeway.

The Core Assessment has now been completed but not yet typed. The thick, thirty-two page document supposedly details the child's developmental needs, the parenting capacity, and the family and environmental factors surrounding the child. Mark and Sean each have their own core assessment, which for the most part has column upon column of questions. This is the ultimate in tick box questionnaires, individuality is not key here, as over two hundred and fifteen lines of tick boxes litter the pages, each with a yes or a no answer.

Occasionally, for a little variety, there are larger boxes with more information and they contain a few sentences. The assessment is clearly intended as a guide and record of the observations that the social worker and family support workers have made. It would be churlish to critisise the assessment too much, as is it only really intended as a tool and not as a judgment, but it clearly shows the amount of paperwork generated during a case such as ours.

In total there are sixty-four pages of core assessment and eighteen pages of parental assessment that have been completed by the time the end of April comes round and in all the recorded visits, assessments and interviews not one person, including the GP and pediatrician involved with Sean's care, have raised a single concern about Sean, Mark or us as their parents.

Now we enter the paradoxical state that will continue until the final hearing. How do you safeguard a child from a danger that you haven't been able to find? How do you work with parents to improve their parenting, when it has been described as excellent? How do you develop strategies to cope with problematical situations when the parents demonstrate they already can? How does the social system help a family who were better able to cope, less stressed, happier and more content before the intervention took place? The system denies that the problem is the system and continues to look to the parents for a confession of perceived guilt and an insight into how to make an imaginary foe disappear.

CHAPTER 18.

At end of the first week in May we meet with our Barrister in her Chambers. The solicitor's advice is to consider the option of each of us having our own legal team. The advantage is that in the event of one of us pointing the finger at the other we would be able to defend ourselves, and in the event of one parent being found guilty the other can fight independently to keep the children.

Darron and I hold our belief that we are parents together and we will defend the accusation together. Darron doesn't believe that I would injure Sean and I don't believe that he would. We talk endlessly about the additional benefits of having more legal advice and support, but we still come back to the same thought. How would a judge view the decision for each parent to be represented separately? Surely there would be an argument for assuming that the parents don't trust one another?

Our solicitor continues to reel off occasions where one parent has turned on the other, normally due to the evidence of a doctor who can make the time frame so specific that it normally incriminates one parent who was in sole care of the baby at the time. I know that the most likely candidate for the lottery of guilt is me and I ask Darron if he would rather that I choose another solicitor for myself. I have barely finished the sentence as he vehemently declines: Whatever happens we will stand together or fall together.

It has been only a few months since we had a similar discussion in our bedroom, only an hour after the first case conference. Whilst we had packed our bags to leave for my mum and dad's we had talked endlessly about the many failings of the system. Up until then we believed, as so many others had before us, that the system would protect the innocent. We thought the accusation would become a bad memory when they met us, spoke to us and saw how child-centred our lives were.

That night, as we crammed clothes into bags we discussed the very real possibility that our children might be taken away and we considered the unthinkable. It seems outlandish now, unbelievable, but it demonstrates how desperate we were as we talked over the possibility of one of us falsely admitting guilt. I tried to reason that if I 'confessed' then Darron would be able to bring the children home and that they wouldn't grow up in care. I can ensure that my family will still support him and be able to see my children in lieu of me.

He rationalised that I would be the better one to care for them, being used to being the main carer and better at domestic tasks and that, of the two of us, he should 'confess'. The problem is that all anyone had mentioned was non-accidental injury and neither of us knew exactly what we were supposed to be confessing to. We had no idea what we would have to admit to doing in order to account for the so called 'injury' and could Social Services be trusted to allow the other parent to bring up the children after such a confession was made?

The conversation came to an end when we both realised that we had been so brow beaten that we were prepared to sacrifice our marriage and our family on the say-so of a single medical report. We vowed that, if we ever bring the children home, we will expose the system for what it is and that, regardless of what it costs us emotionally or financially, we will fight for our children. No one else knows what is best for them, no one else knows their likes and dislikes, their characters and personalities, we alone as parents had taken on that responsibility and we would fight tooth and nail to keep it.

The next court date will be a Case Management Conference (C.M.C.) at Manchester court in mid-May and until this happens the legal process can't move forward. Marie's presence at an advocates' meeting only goes to frustrate everyone involved, as Social Services legal team can't come to any agreement. There is no solid evidence of abuse, on the contrary all those who have met us can see we are dedicated to the welfare of our children, but the accusation is serious and we have no defence against it. It seems that even the Local Authority is unsure how to proceed and we all await the judge's directions at the C.M.C..

As the date for the management conference comes round we are still inundated with visits and appointments. Sean is having regular developmental and follow-up appointments after his discharge from hospital and, combined with the legal meetings and court hearings, life is hectic. Darron and I travel to Manchester by train for the C.M.C. in the hope that the judge will move the case forward but terrified of the whole process all the same.

The court is becoming more familiar now and the initial thoughts I had of being somehow outwardly labeled as a child abuser have lessened, as I reason that everyone in the court is there for different reasons. I wonder how parents such as Sally Clarke coped with both the deaths of her babies and the horrendous public trial which came behind like a tsunami, denying her a chance to grieve and robbing her of her freedom and eventually her life.

I can't imagine facing all this without the strong desire to fight, which comes from having the children to fight for. It is an appalling situation which is only made worse after we take our seats in the courtroom. The judge asks for an update on the case and we are horrified to discover that the whole legal process has ground to a halt. The C.M.C. questionnaires have not been filled in and Derbyshire County Council have not outlined their case.

The case is adjourned for a month as our solicitor and barrister vocalise their frustrations that Derbyshire's legal team seem to need time to build a case that barely has a leg to stand on. Darron and I leave the court upset, the day has been stressful enough and we have had to leave the children with a childminder. I miss them as we walk down the court steps and I fail to see to see how this case could possibly be in the interests of our children. The repeated loss of wages, costs of childcare and stress isn't helping either, as we struggle to pay the train fare home.

The weekend that follows is a relatively uneventful time and as Monday comes round I prepare to take Sean back to the hospital in Stockport for another appointment to see Dr. Fearn. The hospital car park is busy at all times and often it is hard to find a space, leading many people to abandon their cars in unofficial spaces in order to make their various appointments.

Darron parks as I get a ticket for the car and I consider the amount of money we have fed the parking meters since I first got pregnant with Mark. For any outpatient appointment you would be forgiven for thinking an hour would be enough, but the usual delays often take you over that time and then you daren't nip out in case you are called. I decide on two hours, feed the meter coins that roll down and land with a satisfactory clunk and amble back to meet Darron who is getting both Mark and Sean out of the car.

We are kept waiting a while as many parents file in and file out. Sean is weighed and measured and I mention to the nursing staff to check Sean's head circumference. Even in the very early days when Mary Howard led our case, I mentioned the fact that Sean's head circumference had always been large. Since birth, his head circumference had been measured and plotted as on the 75th percentile, yet his height and weight were consistently plotted on the 9th. Unusually, this time when they measure it, his head circumference is magically on the 9th percentile, where it stays thereafter.

Being a person of logic I conclude that Sean doesn't have an abnormally large head, it wouldn't have reduced proportionally with the rest of his measurements at five months of age. Therefore something had made his head large initially and whatever it was had been present since birth. The measurements are plotted and shortly after we are called in to see Sean's consultant, Dr. Fearn.

The small room is bright with lots of stickers and pictures on the walls. It is painted in the usual clinical cream and white with a hospital bed pushed against one wall, a sink and a desk, with the many notes that Sean had amassed in his short life upon it. Dr. Fearn welcomes us with a smile and, after a brief conversation about Sean's progress, his face clouds a little. I listen intently, trying not to react too angrily to the suggestion that another full skeletal x-ray and brain scan might be required.

Ostensibly a paediatrician at a recent conference encouraged his colleagues to repeat x-rays, as on occasion more injuries have been seen after a few weeks. I listen in silence before telling him that we will agree to anything suggested providing he, as Sean's treating physician, recommends it.

Dr. Fearn advises us that, in his opinion, the x-rays would be potentially traumatic and that nobody ever thought there would be anything on the original x-rays anyway. He goes on to state that all the clinicians believed that the only 'evidence' there would ever be would be the bleed on Sean's brain, and that a recent article in the British Medical Journal has proved retinal haemorrhages are not necessarily indicative of shaking either, as he re-iterates that in Sean's case this was never an issue anyway.

Sean is doing well and his development is normal, even advanced in some areas. Dr. Fearn feels that Sean could be discharged if it wasn't for the input of Social Services. I again feel gratitude towards the man who has supported us as parents and genuinely shown care and consideration to our son. In spite of the accusations and recommendations by external agencies he has put Sean's needs and welfare above them all. What more can any parent ask of a doctor than that?

We arrive back from Stockport just in time to give Mark and Sean their dinner before attending the second case conference. The room is the same but it feels a little less tense and we are more resigned to our fate. The case is still in the hands of the legal teams and nobody can move forward while the stale-mate continues.

All the professionals present at the meeting state that they have no concerns about Mark or Sean's welfare, but despite compliments on our excellent standard of care for our children we feel nothing. The children must, we are all told, remain on the 'at risk' register as there is no cause yet known for Sean's injuries. As parents we have no way of knowing if the cause will ever truly be known.

The representatives from Social Services are very different in their tone from those present at the last meeting. Darron and I have not forgotten the demands which followed the case conference last time and we are expecting something similar, yet nothing happens. The meeting takes on a strange feel as phrases such as, "when this is all over and you go home" or "once things return to normal" are said, without reference to the legal battle Social Services have put us in.

Karen, the Health Visitor and our GP request our return to the family home but this request is denied. All those present at the meeting are informed that it will not be possible for us to return home until the cause of Sean's injury has been established and the risk factors understood.

Almost as a footnote we are told that the Crown Prosecution Service will not be pursuing anyone for the injury Sean sustained. The police have closed their case as there isn't any evidence. It is two months since the police interviews and nobody from the police service has contacted us. All we have is the say of Social Services, who claim not to have anything to do with the police investigation. Darron and I have been misled again.

CHAPTER 19.

Caroline, the family resource worker, comes to see us the day after the case conference and her gentle manner is welcomed. I am tired of having to fight and protect my children from the abusive system that has turned our world upside down. We sit across from each other drinking cups of tea and discussing the difference between the way Sean is portrayed on paper and his true mental development.

He is babbling contentedly as Mark 'reads' him books, making up the words to go with the pictures and pausing every now and then to turn the pictures towards Sean. Mark's love of his little brother is absolute and Sean, in return, spends most of his day gazing adoringly at Mark and watching his every move. This is a situation that sometimes replays even today.

Caroline speaks cagily about the court proceedings, not wishing to add to my distress she phrases her questions carefully. I am not distressed by her questions though, on the contrary I am keen to share my views with someone outside the family. Day upon day my mum and dad's house has become like a pressure cooker as all of us try and maintain stability for the children, whilst masking our true feelings of anger and resentment.

Caroline consoles me as I complain about the loneliness I feel, isolated from the village I know, where I could walk to everywhere I needed to go and the solitude at being left in a huge, run-down house in one room. There is no way I can expect my parents to afford to heat the whole house when I am the only one at home, so I stay near the fire. There is no need to go into the other rooms anyway but I miss my bungalow, my child-friendly garden and the neighbours, who had always been a daily source of news and chatter.

I do not share all the negative feelings my family express, I am more pragmatic and thank God daily for the gift of my children and each day I spend with them as their mother. I know that whatever caused the brain hemorrhage Sean suffered he could easily have been left severely disabled or lost his life. I am angry at the accusations but I am not angry with the world.

Karen and Marie also feel my disappointment and annoyance that the court hearing has been adjourned and that proceedings are locked. During one of her visits Marie asks me why we haven't agreed to the instruction of another medical opinion from Dr. Tom Hunter. I don't really know why we are not to accept his opinion, other than it is our solicitor's recommendation that we don't, and so I can't say any more on the matter.

I know that Dr. Hunter is another neuroradiologist and by now I have studied enough previous cases of alleged shaking to know that they will normally agree with one another. Often one expert will defer to the other expert's opinion, particularly if they are specialists in the same field.

Shaken Baby Syndrome has many papers written about it, all detailing the way in which a baby is shaken violently by the care giver and the medical findings that result in such cases. Interestingly, a number of these papers are written by police officers, often senior and retired officers who claim to be able to help fellow officers identify this form of abuse. Doctors refer to each other's work in the field, propping up theories that arise from exchanging similar opinions learnt through 'training' in how to recognize this form of abuse. The lack of bruises and fractures means nothing they claim, in fact it is almost evidential of the fact that the method of abuse was shaking.

If there is no history of psychological illness in the parents or history of harm to any existing children, that is of no consequence, the lack of control is 'understandable' when you are caring for a small demanding baby. They claim that all care givers are bound to be tired and many good care givers lose their temper with a child that does not stop crying; the abuse can be momentary and not intentional.

Of course all this disarms any possible defence provided by loving parents who have no way of proving the abuse didn't happen. Opinions of the evidence are often based on a small number of confessions of abuse by other caregivers in previous cases. The cases normally detail other horrific acts that the perpetrator is guilty of and has confessed to, and they fail to acknowledge that the confessions also include impacts and violence that would obviously account for the injuries without the shaking ever having occurred.

Dr. Tom Hunter will be instructed by the Local Authority and his report will be what they will use to formulate their case. Dr. Timmin's report lies on file, but they are not prepared to adopt it as there are a number of discrepancies. I learn too late that I should never have pointed out the failings of the report and the incorrect facts it contained to Social Services and our social worker. I should instead have made our solicitors force the Local Authority to adopt the report; it is easier to defend against a known entity and the errors and omissions speak volumes.

Instead, in a desperate bid to prove that the accusation was wrong I set about disproving and discrediting the contents and I realise now that they won't make the same mistake again, they will address the flaws in the next report. Marie O'Dwyer speaks to me about Timmin's report and states that there is no other evidence of any harm other than the possibility of alleged shaking. If Dr. Hunter maintains the same likely cause then the Local Authority will proceed with its case, if not then they will have to re-think their position.

I know that in all likelihood the two doctors will stand together, I know that Dr. Timmin's report is being sent with Sean's scans and therefore Dr. Hunter will not be writing from a blank page. I can only wait and hope that Dr. Hunter is more open minded and that all the factors we have mentioned will be considered but, in truth, I don't hold out much hope.

As the summer fast approaches I make the decision to go back to work. I had planned to take unpaid leave after my maternity leave ends but this is no longer an option. The increased costs of paying for a house we don't live in, the travel costs to various court hearings and the loss of Darron's shift pay every time he takes time off, means that our finances are dire. Anyone with two children will know that the bills increase and we are constantly asked to attend meetings and arrange some form of childcare.

With my parents both working full time and my grandma having already done enough, we frequently rely on a childminder, which is an expense we don't need, with only one wage coming in. The washable nappies I had used with Mark are left unused, as it is impossible to add them to my parents' laundry and ours with only one machine and the need for two lots of nappies.

This leads me to part with my principles and use disposables in order to make life easier but it also adds to the expense. This particular decision leads to a very amusing situation on my first day back at work, when I come home to find Mark wearing a nappy that barely fastens at the front and Sean in one that is almost at his armpits! Darron is not at all pleased at my constant giggles as I advise him of his mistake, huffing he replies "At least I tried!"

Work soon becomes my respite and I start to have time to myself again. I have worked at the local pharmacy since Mark was born, having been unable to return to the male-dominated world of IT with a small baby. The job is ideal as it is just a short walk from home and with the customers being local, I had soon learnt most of their names. My work colleagues are aware of the situation as I have frequently kept them informed on my regular trips to pick up Sean's prescriptions. They listen as I complain about the system and attempt to make helpful suggestions that help only in the fact they are a display of support.

I find it difficult at times to see new mums with their babies, complaining of lack of sleep or some trivial issue that isn't important, as I compare their lives to mine. However, there are times when I serve customers who are seriously and even terminally ill and I thank my lucky stars that I'm not in their shoes. I console family members as they return prescriptions for destruction from relatives who have passed away and see the parents of children, who are severely disabled, collect medications with a smile. Life, I thought to myself, isn't fair but it is what you make of it. There are days when the court case and Social Services never leave my mind and there are days when I am happy and hopeful that life will soon return to normal.

I am helped in my optimistic attitude by making arrangements for Sean's Christening. It had occurred to us to have him baptised in hospital but he had rallied and we had decided that we would hold a family Christening once he was discharged. On Sunday 30th May, Sean is baptised in the same church in which we married. The local priest had been such a help during Sean's initial illness and we had knelt before the altar on many occasions praying that he would make it and here he was dressed in his cream jacket and trousers embroidered with gold. The families have all gathered and for one day we are able just to be a normal family. Mark behaves perfectly throughout and Sean, who has always loved water, doesn't even cry.

The start of June leads to new worries about Sean's health as he is sick repeatedly sometimes with a vengeance and accompanying it is a very strange lump. I take Sean to the

GP but the lump is not visible when she looks and I wonder if I am now imagining things, but she reassures me and asks me to monitor Sean closely. I return home but Sean is sick and in the nights and no longer sleeps through.

I am back at work now and the sleeplessness leaves me tired. I ask the health visitor, who is due to call anyway, to take a closer look. Darron and I have both seen the lump and the previous night my parents had seen it too. Something isn't right and I start to feel panicky that we will be blamed if something is wrong. Karen weighs Sean again and confirms that he has not gained weight in three weeks and I advise her he is getting worse.

Darron takes Sean to see the GP again, as we are both unhappy with the way he is behaving, believing that Sean may have a hernia. Mark has already had a hernia repaired and Sean's symptoms look so similar that the GP refers us to Pendlebury. It is not what we want to hear. Pendlebury hospital has come to represent the very darkest hours of our lives and neither of us want to return there, asking instead if we might be able to take him to another hospital. Karen mentions the possibility of taking Sean to Sheffield instead but as we consider asking for a new referral, Pendlebury contact us with an appointment for the following day.

Darron and I are both supposed to be meeting with the Guardian the following day and call to ask him if we can reschedule. Isaac tells us that the childrens welfare is obviously the most important thing and that he will arrange a visit after the next court hearing. I hang up the phone knowing we will be going back into our old nightmare.

The appointment is with the same consultant we had seen for Mark's hernia and there is no reason for us to be anxious but the feeling in the car, as we make the journey, is tense. We both remember the last time we set foot in the hospital at Pendlebury, Manchester and the memory is still raw. I have already had to call up Social Services' offices and advise them of the change in our plans - everything now involves phone calls and messages as even appointments have to be verified and confirmed.

We hope that the reception we get this time will be more amiable than before and, as the appointment is in the main hospital, away from the mental health ward, it feels like a different building. The air feels fresh and the rooms are bright and airy. Sean's consultant tells us that Sean's hernia must be repaired quickly as it may be becoming strangulated. I am glad we persisted in getting help and I feel safe in the consultant's hands as she explains everything fully and makes arrangements for an admission as soon as possible. There is a marked difference in the way we are being treated as parents without the shadow of accusation or the whispers of child abuse.

The following days pass without any incident as we ready ourselves for another trip to Manchester High Court. The court is becoming familiar to us, almost like going to the library or the school gates. We arrive expecting to be searched and walk through the body scanners having left our metal objects on the trays provided. Darron has learnt from the mistake of his first court visit and has removed the small pen knife that normally resides on his key ring.

The knife is tiny, more of a novelty than a working tool, burgundy red with a tiny one inch blade, the only useful purpose I had ever found for it was to cut string. To the court security guards it is still classed as a weapon and it had been confiscated for collection as we left the court. It now sits safely on my mum's kitchen table as neither of us wants to raise any more attention to ourselves than is strictly necessary.

If it wasn't for the reason for our attendance at court I could become very interested in the coming and goings that happen there. The large number of robed and wigged people who sweep about with bundles of papers, often tied up with what appears to be ribbon, are interspersed with a whole cross-section of society. At any one time, as the court clerks call the names of those requested to enter a particular court there are a number of people waiting in the corridors. Some, like us, look pensive and worried, others cock-sure, and occasionally there is a commotion and outburst because of a finding or outcome. The court staff look almost bored as they confirm the attendance of those listed and check that all parties are present before the hearings commence.

We have returned to the court for the rescheduled Case Management Conference (C.M.C.). Another month has gone by, with us living full time at my parents, and this hearing will still not change our day-to-day living arrangements, as we await the judge's direction on the medical experts. We file in to the court in a resigned fashion as the Local Authority barrister, a loud woman who looks remarkably like a brusque scout leader with high heels, marches in before us.

We have no need to be first and so we hover at the back uncertainly. Our solicitor, Julie, points to two seats next to her and we sit down watching and listening but unable to comment. One of the most difficult things I have encountered so far during the case, is the inability to comment. Darron and I must listen to aspersions and allegations that the Local Authority claims 'are presented to them' and yet we can say nothing. We rely on our solicitor but we are constantly told that our evidence and submissions will have to wait for the final hearing.

Meanwhile, the judge makes an order that the Local Authority are to write a letter of instruction to their new witness, Dr. Tom Hunter, by the 6th July and directs that it must be received and filed with the court by July 18th. That marks the end of the long awaited C.M.C. and all that happens now is we wait some more.

CHAPTER 20.

As the end of June arrives I am allowed to spend some time at home with the children: A few precious hours to play house. The move is a step forward on the face of it but it feels nonsensical as we know we would never hurt either of our children. I am allowed two short afternoons in my own garden and I make the most of it, as my parents' house has no real garden, being very much a renovation project. I have missed being able to leave the conservatory doors open and let Mark come and go as he pleases.

Our garden at home is fenced in and the dog too can wander freely, sniffing the lilies and investigating the rockery for the sign of any intruders, no matter how small. Mark has a swing, a slide, a water table and a sand pit and we all enjoy the wooden summerhouse that Mark loves to play in. The lawn is ever so slightly sloped, but not hugely so, and Mark can easily spend a large amount of time on the grass kicking a ball or climbing on the small bouncy castle that is tethered to the fence.

We have designed our garden carefully and it is meant for children, unlike the gravel and hard landscaping my parents have, which is meant for minimal maintenance and two working adults. I pine the loss of my home for Mark and Sean as much as for me. I can't help feeling that we have all been deprived as I feel the summer sun on my back and think of the time we could have enjoyed as a family. I mourn the time we have lost and often wonder if our lives will ever be normal again.

Sean's hernia repair is scheduled for the 6th July and he is expected to remain in hospital overnight. The date comes around surprisingly quickly and the morning is busy as we prepare, leaving Mark with my grandma again. Sean is unsettled as he has been starved ready for his operation and the two hour journey round the motorway is a noisy one, as he cries wanting his breakfast.

He is six months old and he hasn't gained any weight over the last month and we worry for him as we arrive, find the ward and he is admitted for his operation. Darron and I look around edgily, speculating what is written in Sean's notes. We are unsure how we will be treated and I feel sick to my stomach putting Sean's life back in their hands but I have no choice.

I hand over the endocarditis warning card that I have been given in relation to the hole in his heart and the medics murmur to each other as they search through his notes for mention of it. I make a sarcastic statement to Darron, out of earshot of the doctors, that if there wasn't so much finger pointing and there weren't so many accusatory reports they might be able to find important medical information in his notes.

Regardless of everything we have endured, any parent who has had to see their child go through an operation feels helpless. As I carry him into theatre and kiss him on the cheek I cried with worry as the anaesthetic takes hold and he falls completely silent. His tiny body looks so fragile again under all the machines but he has to have the hernia repaired; if it strangulated it would be too dangerous. Sean is nowhere near a year old and he is going through a general anaesthetic yet again and there is nothing we, as parents, can do but carry on waiting.

The surgery goes really well and the consultant confirms what we had seen, with regards to the size and position of the lump, as being exactly what she had found.

This had made the repair a lot easier and, if he is well enough, he may be able to go home in the evening. Sean sleeps for several hours as we watch children go into surgery and come back flanked with nurses and parents. The nurses usually carry the notes and blood pressure monitors and the parents carry balloons and cuddly toys.

It is after lunchtime when Sean wakes up and he has barely opened his eyes when the screaming starts. The nurses check his chart for pain medication and administer it as soon as they can but still he seems unsettled and unhappy. The nurses are kind and helpful, one even returns a purse to me that I had left on Sean's bed, fearing it might be taken. I thank her before revealing to her that it contains nothing intrinsically valuable, only a set of my mum's rosary beads and a set of my own.

That day, like every day we went to court I carried three sets of rosary beads - mine, my mum's and a set belonging to my aunty, left to me after she died. I had taken one set with me and left the others on the bed, they are not worth stealing but I was grateful for the thought and consideration.

Sean cries continually for half and hour, creating fear that he may burst his stitches. Darron and I are in no doubt as to what the problem is and we tell the staff on the ward that we don't think it is pain that is making him scream. Sean had endured far more painful procedures and he tolerated pain well, what he didn't tolerate was hunger. Even today Sean can't miss a meal. In fact if he eats one meal late he still reminds you when the next meal is due - food and Sean are synonymous!

The nurses claim that, in their experience, most babies aren't hungry after they have been to theatre: We aren't convinced. In a move that was probably to pacify us more than Sean, they provide us with a bottle of water. This keeps Sean happy for a minute or two and the ward returns to a calm environment briefly, until he spits the water out and resumes his loud demonstrations. Looking at each other, the nurse and ward sister consider allowing him some sugar water and, against all usual regulations, they tell us that if he waits fifteen minutes they will get him some.

Five minutes of screaming later they yield, the sister returning with the sugar water and exclaiming that she is breaking the guidelines and that he will probably be sick. The sugar water lasts even less time than the water, as Sean quickly realises he is being fobbed off. He has been without food for the longest amount of time in his life thus far and he isn't at all happy about it. His fine features and round face, which normally show off his large orb like eyes and downy hair, are screwed up as he contorts with rage, the volume escalating with each passing minute.

Darron and I stare at the medical staff, imploring them to do something as what feels like every person on the ward glares at the baby making all the noise. The doctor on the ward comes over expressing concern that if Sean continues to cry so forcefully he will potentially rupture the stitches that are holding his wound together. I again put forward the suggestion that it is unlikely he will stop crying until he gets what he wants and he wants food.

With great reluctance it is agreed that he can have his bottle of milk under supervision of the nurse and they agree with each other that it is more than likely he will be sick within minutes. 9oz of milk later and Sean falls fast asleep, worn out by the crying and knocked for six by the anaesthetic. The saying goes that mother knows best but I'd hate to brag.

Sean is discharged within the hour and we are travelling home with him snoozing soundly in the back of the car. Relief sweeps through me and I find myself feeling tired as the emotion of the day ebbs away. The day has been a stepping stone in recovering our faith in the hospital and the staff who work there. We have been kept informed, we have been treated with respect and we have been able to communicate with the staff, giving them vital information that they had failed to see in the plethora of notes.

I can't retell here in words just how scared I was walking up the hospital steps, reliving a time when our baby was under the protection of the very people, who were letting him down and knowing that I could do nothing to change it. I remember the night I walked down the hospital drive having been told that Sean was suspected as having been injured whilst in our care to hear a man at the bus stop say to me, "Cheer up love it might never happen!" only for me to burst into tears and retaliate: "It already has."

Within days Sean was happier and more settled than he had been in weeks. For the second time I felt vindicated that I had insisted that there had been a problem and it wouldn't be the last time I would have to insist on action. Sean, still blissfully unaware of the circus surrounding him, impresses everyone with his recovery to the point that within weeks he demonstrates it by trying to stand up. Mark enjoys Sean's new found skill and constantly tries to encourage him to perch on anything to hand. I am delighted that Sean is developing at a rate of knots and he in turn revels in the additional attention as Darron and I clap loudly at any new achievement.

Mark is now causing concern with his difficulty in talking. His words are part formed and hard to understand. Several times it is suggested to me that perhaps he should have speech therapy. I am open to the idea in principle but feel that we should first get his hearing checked, knowing that hearing problems can cause speech difficulties. I notice that Mark never watches cartoons, he only watches television if real people are on it and even then he shows very little interest unless they talk directly to camera.

I start to notice that he ignores me if he has his back to me and he uses the baby signs I had taught him as a tiny baby more and more. I am constantly informed that Mark's speech would be nowhere near as good as it is if he has hearing problems and that he simply couldn't pronounce words correctly. In the end at the next case conference I formally request that a hearing test be undertaken and I ensure that the request is minuted.

In spite of being made to feel, yet again, that I am a neurotic or disillusioned mum, I am justified when the test reveals Mark's hearing is virtually non-existent. The clinician is amazed that Mark had learnt to speak so well and Mark in turn shocks us all by demonstrating that he can lip-read. When will the medical profession start to accept that parents know their own children? I had been sure that Mark's problems were related to his hearing and I had now spent seven months getting rebuffed.

Within a few weeks of Mark's first operation he was making leaps and bounds with his speech and no longer referred to himself as 'Mart'. Darron was thrilled when I spent an entire afternoon either side of our patio doors persuading Mark to breath on the glass so that he could figure out how to say 'h'. The world was his oyster as 'orses' became 'horses' and 'ats' became 'hats'. Mark had been promised a bicycle bell as a reward if he succeeded and, as Darron returned with him from the bike shop and fixed the bell to his bike, he rang it incessantly, proving both his ability to hear it and the pride of his latest accomplishment.

I can't remember my birthday that year or Darron's. Things like that no longer seemed to matter as July was taken up with the anticipation of Dr. Tom Hunter's report. It would be this report that would decide if we could go home again or if we would have to fight on in a family court, where the evidence need only prove more likely than not.

We wait and wait as the date comes and goes without news. By the next court hearing on 3rd September it is apparent that, despite the judge's directions, Dr. Hunter hasn't even been instructed and will therefore not be able to produce a report until mid-October. Following the adverse publicity surrounding shaking cases, other experts that have been approached have declined to undertake the work and this now leaves all the other medical questions unanswered.

As autumn comes around and the leaves fall we are surprised to make a sudden leap forward. In September 2004, five months after we have been forced out of our home we are allowed to go back. This is on the proviso that neither Darron nor I are allowed to remain in the house on our own with the children. When Darron works nights I will still have to pack up all our things and stay at my parents' and we will still have to spend weekends there as there are no professionals available to visit us. Our nomadic existence is not ideal but we grab the chance to begin the move home.

The change is proposed on the grounds that Marie, in one hundred and five visits, has never had any concerns over the well being of our children or the quality of our parenting. Mark is also featured in the proposed plan as being more at ease in his own home and a conclusion made that our home is more suitable for a family having secure play space and everything to hand. The news brings a welcome reprieve from the fraught situation of the previous months but we still await the next report. The ongoing court case is a constant reminder that we are at the mercy of the system and our hopes are dashed in a single sentence: 'He agrees with Timmin.'

It was like an old wound being ripped open again: all the emotions that we had started to suppress, the anger, the bitterness and the disbelief came flooding back to the surface. Marie didn't stay long as she left the new report for us to read, there was nothing to say. In effect, the evidence wasn't any different, the opinion merely someone else's, but the rug had been pulled from under us again on the say so of another medical 'expert'.

CHAPTER 21.

Hunter's report is wordy and much lengthier than it's predecessor. I wonder if this is because this one has been fully paid for. A report for a court hearing can cost thousands of pounds and yet most of the experts are commenting on medical findings, not discovering a cure for some exotic disease. Perhaps, if we paid more for the research required, we may not need to pay so much for opinion. Heaven forbid that anyone could suggest that, with investment in the right research, opinion could one day be replaced with fact.

Contradictory statements form the backbone of most of the report, with a suitable amount of definitive answers, then seemingly retracted with information that stated he couldn't be sure. The words 'usually', 'cannot see', 'suggestion of', 'maybe' and 'could represent' were used repeatedly and yet it would be enough to jeopordise the future of our family. The numbers of research papers pinned to the back of the report are plentiful but they are chosen carefully. I could append similar such evidence against such a diagnosis of shaken baby syndrome but I am not the expert.

Experts are those asked for their opinion on matters that can't be scientifically proven, the definition of opinion being: A belief or conclusion held with confidence but not substantiated by positive knowledge or proof. Simply, they only have to believe it is true. Dr. Fieldman would eventually defend his position and his career, having provided a definitive cause of shaking to a judge, only for the cause to be found to be a natural one.

The basis of such reports is inferential, doctors constantly stating alternative explanations for subdural bleeds and then ruling them out categorically, with constant references and phrases such as 'extremely unlikely'. The point I would like to make is that, by definition, if you prosecute enough parents some will fall into this hallowed 'unlikely category', but this possibility fails to get a mention.

In our case alone I could quote that the Cholestasis I suffered in pregnancy affects only 1% of mothers, the pre-eclampsia occurs in 2-3% of pregnancies and the incidence of storage pool disorder is thought to affect 1 in 1000 people in the UK giving fractions of a percent as the statistical likelihood. I am sure you would conclude that in our case, rare and unlikely was the norm.

Dr. Hunter concludes that Sean could have suffered from more than one subdural haematoma, thereby inferring more than one episode of abuse. He emphatically maintains that the "relative twisting of the brain and skull causing rupture of the small blood vessels *usually* involves a considerable degree of force such as a traffic accident or shaking". Yet several pages later he also claims that it is not clear what degree of force is required to inflict these injuries on infants.

Dr. Hunter omits to mention that recent scientific evidence has shown that it may not be necessary to shake an infant violently to produce such injuries. Earlier the very same year we had eagerly read the March issue of the medical journal 'The Lancet' in which there was a discussion about research that was looking into whether or nor subdural haematomas could be related to birth. Over eight percent of the babies scanned had a subdural haematoma that clearly did not relate to a car crash or shaking during labour. The target group was small and therefore the research could be glossed over by those determined to maintain their definitive opinions, but it was a start.

Medical professionals are right to be wary about offering a possible defence to child abusers, who will obviously rely on any defence possible, even if they are guilty. However, if none of the clinicians believe the child has been abused and none of the interviews, assessments or threats uncovers any reason or marker of abuse, why are the parents still hounded? Dr Hunter states in his report that we, as parents, "Provided no history of accidental trauma of sufficient severity to account for Sean's injuries". Fourteen pages further into the report he then states that the force required is unknown.

The report, written for the court as evidence, is full of statements that read as fact, but with a critical eye and perseverance you can read through the aspersions and see the obvious flaws. The crucial flaw being that there are no concrete facts because there has never been enough research.

Several times Dr. Hunter refers to a bleed in Sean's brain which he thinks could have been there for at least three weeks, possibly longer. He then writes that in his opinion the trauma must have happened as soon as Sean's behaviour changed on the day of his admission, giving rise to the possibility of him being shaken at mother and baby group in a room full of witnesses. In fact the time he provides for the alleged assault is very precise even though it is only based on Sean's behaviour.

Dr. Hunter consistently words his report from a standpoint of non-accidental injury. He never once alludes to the fact that some of the findings he is actually making reference to, are true about any subdural bleed. Behaviour changes would be expected for any patient with a brain haemorrhage, but he does not make that clear in his report. Yet, if subdural bleeds always lead to a significant change in behaviour, how can there ever be older bleeds that nobody has noticed? If Dr. Hunter is correct, how would there be a bleed older than three weeks that had gone unnoticed by the midwife and health visitor?

These questions are easily addressed by Dr. Hunter, by making reference to the fact that heath visitors, midwives and GP's do not have sufficient training in the area of non-accidental (deliberate) injury, to recognise it when they see it. That specialism is reserved for those so high up the tree that they can be arrogant enough to believe that they alone know best. Common sense is not a strong point in this instance.

Dr. Hunter's report doesn't even countenance that accidental injuries can cause such bleeding, despite the fact that in 2001 an American doctor studied childhood head injuries caused by falls and concluded that fatalities can occur from a short-distance fall. Sean was too young to have had a fall and we only ever changed him on the floor and never put him on our bed unattended, but other parents have been prosecuted on the false assumption that 'babies bounce'.

Children are able to survive high falls without injury it is true, Darron once witnessed a very young child fall two floors from a tower block balcony. Having heard an almighty thud he reluctantly ran to see if there was anything he could do, only to hear the child call to his siblings and run back up the stairs! His mother having not witnessed the accident would have been unable to prove the incident if the boy had later fallen ill.

The famous case of Natasha Richardson, wife of Liam Neeson, who injured her head in a skiing accident, raised public awareness that head injury can be a delayed killer. Natasha, following a fall during a beginners skiing lesson, went back in to her hotel room to rest. She had refused medical attention twice but was taken to hospital hours later with a headache and died the following day of a brain haemorrhage.

Dr Hunter's report refers to a baby that nobody has had concerns about, failing to take account of the fact that we had raised concerns directly with the health visitor and midwife. We had made three logged calls to the hospital in the days leading up to Sean's admission, but these calls are not referred to. There is no mention of the dangers to babies of obstetric cholestasis, no mention of the lack of vitamin K after birth and no reference to the additional medication I was prescribed, some of which I later found to be unlicensed.

I had also been advised to take low dose aspirin during pregnancy in order to prevent miscarriage and avoid pre-eclampsia and years later I would find out that this could have been catastrophic for Sean and myself as we both have bleeding conditions and aspirin is known to exacerbate bleeding.

Dr. Hunter follows the mantra as he states there is evidence of retinal haemorrhages in both eyes, failing to add in his report to the court that these had been considered to be four weeks old in a baby that was only a little over three weeks at the time, meaning that they related to birth. In fact a number of babies display such findings after birth and babies born with inherited bleeding disorders will often demonstrate such findings.

The paper starts to anger me as I read line upon line of differing opinion. The suggested fact is that all subdural haematomas are rare after accidents but common in non-accidental trauma. Surely if the idea of an accident or other medical evidence is ruled out and parents and caregivers are constantly accused of non-accidental injury there are potentially hundreds of children out there, like Sean, with undiagnosed conditions that are left untreated because the cause has been incorrectly attributed to shaking.

If the complex medical evidence and a string of contributory factors are never investigated and subdural bleeds are always classed as non-accidental unless proven otherwise, doctors will go on making a diagnosis of cause rather than one of medical condition. Once the baby or child has left hospital and their notes read non-accidental trauma the medical profession add the statistic to the next court report they write. It follows that age old adage that 'a cow has four legs therefore all animals with four legs are cows.' The prophecy is self fulfilling.

Hunter refutes any other possible evidential papers or new findings by stating "Whilst this may be the case...the radiological and opthamological evidence is based on observational studies and deemed to be N.A.I." Dr. Hunter appears to hold the view that the study of radiology provides proven evidence. Interestingly the report by his colleague Dr. Timmin shows differences of opinion despite the fact that both opinions are based on the only scan ever taken of Sean at that point. Dr. Timmin's description varies as to what he thinks he is seeing and his prognosis is dire. Dr. Hunter has the benefit of knowing that he is offering an opinion on a baby who is developing normally. His report therefore demonstrates different findings and a more positive outcome.

It must be remembered that both doctors are commenting on the same scan, the evidence can't have changed if the image is the same, surely? Their differing professional opinion is simply that, both doctors hold different views of what the scan means, their interpretations are different. There is no alteration of the facts or a difference in the 'evidential' scan image. In the murder trial of another mother, Dr. Fieldman and Dr. Hunter would take opposite sides of the argument, both reading different meaning into the same radiological 'evidence'. Clearly the 'radiological and opthamological evidence' is not evidence at all, merely interpretation.

The report has given Derbyshire County Council's legal team the evidence they require to return to court. Initially, their reasons for care proceedings were shaky with no firm basis in fact, with the judge's constant questioning about what their position actually is. The position is made clear as I read the report and know immediately that we will be going to war over it. In the years that follow, I often wonder if we had fought harder initially, would the case have been thrown out?

I will never know.

While we have spent so much time defending our current position and trying as best as we can to shield our children from our distress and the difficult situation we are in, the Local Authority have been trawling for more evidence in which to prove they had a right to do what they had already done. Our human rights to liberty, freedom of expression, peaceful enjoyment of our property and the freedom of assembly and association have all been called into question. There were a further two basic human rights, enshrined in UK law that there was no question we had been denied; we have been denied the respect for our private and family life and the right to a fair trial.

CHAPTER 22.

I believe that if I can see the holes in the report, Social Services will too, but it won't matter. The court only has to be satisfied that it is more likely than not, that Sean has been injured deliberately and/or that because of this we have failed to protect him. The court's decision will be based on the 'evidence' put before it and our legal team seems to be unable to get any answers to the questions we have asked with regard to Sean's medical history.

The visits from Marie are more difficult following the release of Dr. Hunter's report. Up until this time our relationship with her has been somewhat relaxed, without the initial constant changes in restrictions and threats issued by her predecessor. Now Marie observes in her notes that my attitude is petulant in the face of the 'increasing' evidence, which, as far as Darron and I are concerned, purely constitutes an additional report from an expert in exactly the same specialism as that of Dr. Timmin.

Social Services appear unable to see that the evidence is an educated opinion based on the radiological findings. These doctors are not specialists in neonatal care, blood disorders or birth. My obstetrician submits a report stating that there are a number of cases of birth-related subdural haematomas and brain injury due to lack of oxygen and other factors but it appears to carry no weight.

Karen has contacted Birmingham Women's Hospital, who send an article referring to a brain haemorrhage suffered by a baby in the womb. The mother had been diagnosed with obstetric cholestasis and there was thought to be a link. It seems that any medical evidence we try to introduce is summarily dismissed as the desperate attempts of guilty parents to exonerate themselves, or is not relevant due to the fact that the radiologist's report, which stretched to numerous pages, invariably addressed a number of other possible causes by giving the reasons why he dismissed them.

It transpires that the neuroradiologists are easily able to comment on other medical factors covering a multitude of different specialisms, giving the impression of an almost Godlike existence.

The latter part of 2004 is spent in increasing frustration as I watch my family start to buckle under the strain. Sean is increasingly mobile as his first birthday approaches and it is getting harder for us to give him the freedom we had afforded Mark. I am still tied to staying in the presence of another adult if I am at home and therefore I am lacking any kind of personal space. In Mark's infancy I had enjoyed walking the dog for miles over the fields, talking to him in his baby sling and taking in the views of the Derbyshire hills, but I can't expect Grandma to join me.

If I stay at my parents' house, when they get home from working full time they are tired and the winter light is fading. Neither my home nor theirs can afford me the lifestyle that I have been used to. I am a working mother of two children under three and I am expected to meet lists of requirements whilst still providing my children with stability and hiding the constant feelings of anger and hurt.

The children are unable to go out for the day with me because we have to be present for the visitors that are still arriving each day and the requirement that I must go to the baby groups I have always attended with Mark is difficult because I am often still staying at my parent's house. Marie tries her best to facilitate transport arrangements but even if I had been able to drive, I wouldn't be able to take them alone.

I am now given a weekly planner so that I can meet with all the visits and meetings and a list of where the children are expected to be on any given day. Having always been an organised person, I feel aggrieved at the insinuation that I am unable to remember my own weekly arrangements and upset that I have to attend various playgroups and toddler groups regardless of how I am feeling.

On one particular day I am in tears as Karen arrives. I have struggled to make up bottles for Sean, get Mark ready, make calls to the social worker and solicitor and fit in the early morning visit that was the only available time on offer for a health visitor, who had a whole list of mothers to support. I have been up at various times in the night as Sean has been unsettled and I feel like clingfilm stretched too thin.

Karen has gone the extra mile, travelling twelve miles out of her way to see me at my parents' house, and not just because Social Services have asked her to. I look on her as a companion and friend and rely on her for reassurances about Sean's day to day development and progress. I know that she could refuse to visit, it is not the job of the health visitor to monitor parents in this way, but as she comforts me her support is invaluable. The authorities have taken a capable mother and turned her into a paranoid mess.

I am unsure as I write this if I should confess to what is now happening in our day-to-day lives. Darron, who has been back at work since Sean came home from hospital, is struggling to deal with the intrusions, feeling that somehow he has failed as a father and husband in protecting us all. He now spends very little time communicating and will often sit and stare at a blank wall. The GP has prescribed anti-depressants and Darron is trying his best to provide for the family and drive me to all Sean and Mark's appointments.

For my part, I feel put upon, it is my life that is affected most by the constant visitors, it is me who has to re-run everything every time a question is asked. It is my day to day routine that is set out in the weekly planner we are handed and as time goes on, we start to retreat into our own separate worlds, functioning on a day by day basis but no more than that.

Darron has been experiencing a whole host of symptoms and is being treated for a bad back. We both feel that stress is playing its part and don't think too much about it, as there is no point. I am also struggling with gynaecological problems, which I have had since Sean's birth and I am waiting for tests at the hospital as I am regularly bleeding heavily without cause. We both just exist.

With all the sleepless nights, visits and stress I was also getting more worrying symptoms. For a while I had been imagining terrible things happening to Sean. Strange, scary and realistic visions of awful accidents, Sean falling down the stairs, me treading on him, Sean tipping out of his seat, Sean being grabbed by strangers in the park or something heavy landing on him. I keep these thoughts to myself, convinced that if I share them my children will be taken away. The images haunt me more during the day and come to me whilst I am in the middle of the most mundane tasks.

It gets so bad that if I need to walk past Sean and he is crawling or playing on his play mat, I will virtually pass him on the opposite side of the room. When I pick Sean up I try not to lift him, I just slide him gently onto my bent knees and raise him with my legs underneath him and my hands around his middle. I am not sure what the visions mean but I feel that I am finally losing my grip on reality. My marriage and husband are suffering and my children deserve better but I am trapped and I am all they have.

Darron is increasingly getting pain in his lower back, which has now become so bad that at times he rolls around the floor in absolute agony. I beg him to make an appointment with the GP but he refuses, not wanting to add any more appointments to the list and confident that the situation will resolve.

I speak urgently in hushed tones with my mum and

dad in the kitchen of their home as to what might be wrong, as they have both suffered from bad backs and arthritis and the way Darron is contorting would be virtually impossible. We decide that he must go back to the doctor; we all feel certain that it isn't his back that is causing the pain.

Darron and I go back to work the following day, having dropped the children off at the childminder's house. The morning goes fairly quickly and as I am considering how I am going to persuade Darron to see the GP, the phone rings. Neither of us ever calls the other at work unless there is an emergency, so I am surprised to find my husband on the end of the line.

He speaks quietly, in between gasped breaths, as he tells me that he has collapsed at work and has been taken to the doctor's surgery. I am left awaiting news but it does not take long as Darron is admitted to hospital within the hour. Not being able to drive and still at work, my boss asks me if I want to leave there and then. No matter how much I want to, I can't. I am not allowed to sleep at home without another person present, and now Darron has been admitted to hospital I will be in contravention of the agreement unless I move. I am unable to take the children anywhere that isn't part of the plan and I can't get them back to my parents without help.

In the end I telephone my grandma, who takes me home to pack my bags and picks up the children so that we can travel to my parents' house and await further news. I am reeling at the suddenness, the shock preventing me from feeling anything but numb. How much more can our family take?

I travel to see Darron the next day, taking two buses and walking a distance to the hospital. By now the doctors have confirmed that the pain is coming from his kidney and the area is swollen. Darron's ward is full of older gentlemen who take a great deal of delight in teasing their latest victim. Whilst test after test takes place, Darron is denied food and drink and his fellow patients take turns to tear pictures of food from their newspapers and leave them tantilisingly on his bed. The humour is a welcome relief for me, if not so funny for Darron!

Their banter and joviality make the experience more bearable but as Darron is wheeled off for yet more tests I try to corner the nurse. I have spent enough time in hospital to know that the medical staff have an idea what the problem might be. I can see them cast repeated glances in our direction and their overly kind manner is a little worrying as they chastise the other patients for taunting Darron.

I decide to press for information but in a short time I wish that I had. There is a very large mass over the area of his left kidney and it is this that has been causing the blood in his urine for the past year. I persist for further details until the nurse finally gives in acknowledging their suspicions but unable to be certain. "We don't normally see these problems in people so young, the mass is large and we can only think of one cause…" She trails off and her head drops as I ask; "You think it's cancer?"

The nurse looks back at me with a sympathetic smile as her face confirms what she has hinted. Darron is still having tests and there is no way I can tell him, what is the point of worrying him if the diagnosis isn't conclusive? I fix on the happy bright face that I have used so many times in the months before, determined to stay strong and wait for my husband to come back to me.

That night, as I leave him on the ward, I look to the sky thinking, "why us?" No answer comes back and for a minute I consider what good my faith is to me, but it is too late, my faith is all I have. I arrive back through the door of my parents' home with my happy face on; I play with the children and change them into their PJ's. The phone rings and I answer it in passing. "Heather?" It is Marie's voice on the other end of the line and she sounds worried. It occurs to me that we have

165

missed our visit in the rush and, in trying to meet with their restrictions, I have not let her know where I am.

Tired and exhausted I have to relay the events of the day in order to explain why I am no longer where I am scheduled to be. Marie's voice softens as she reassures me that she is sure everything will be alright and I thank her almost automatically as I hang up the phone. A thought occurs to me in seconds and I pick up the receiver again and dial the ward number. I know it isn't a normal request but the nurse agrees to get Darron to the phone and as he answers I let Mark yell "Night, night Daddy!"

The next two days pass in a blur of hospital visits and Social Services calls. On the second day, I take the children to see their dad in the hospital, Mark keen to ride on a double decker and Sean happily sleeping due to the rhythmic motion of the bus. The journey is longer with the children by my side and carrying Sean from the bus stop I am surprised by how big he has grown of late. The only thing that keeps me going, is that if they give Darron a diagnosis of cancer, then I am going to give him something to fight for. As the odds again seem to stack up against us, Darron and I start to turn to each other again, safe in the knowledge that whatever happens we will face it together.

The news comes as a shock in more ways than one. Darron has been on the ward for several days, when the nephrologist comes to speak to him, asking questions about his family and past history before informing us that he has polycystic kidney disease. The disease is a condition in which the kidneys grow many cysts which gradually replace the healthy tissue, leading eventually to kidney failure and the necessity for a transplant. Darron's kidneys are twice the normal size and will grow still further as the condition worsens but it isn't cancer.

The nephrologist hopes that with the right treatment Darron can live a normal life for many years, providing he takes care of his health and treats his sky-high blood pressure.

The bleeding and pain have been caused by some of the larger cysts rupturing but, with a prescription collected from the pharmacy I am allowed to take him home. Darron has now joined the ranks of the unlikely, being diagnosed with a condition affecting 0.0002% of the population.

CHAPTER 23.

Julie, the solicitor we have instructed, now starts to back track. In our next meeting she tells us of another family, whose child had been found with an unexplained broken leg. Social Services had been called in and the parents have been asked to explain the injury, detailing a minor fall. The case has been brought to court and Julie is representing the father who has been directly accused.

Whilst questioning the father it soon transpired that some of the father's family had brittle bone disease and their symptoms were similar to that of the small child. Julie tells us that, because of this, the father had been pressing for the child to be tested but the doctors were refusing. She had then contacted a medical expert, who agreed that the break, as per the paperwork she had provided to him, could easily be attributed to brittle bone disease and had verbally offered to write a report stating as much.

Unfortunately, the doctor had subsequently called back to check who had written the original medical report, the one the Local Authority was using. He then had a sudden change of heart and backed out of the case, declaring that he couldn't 'go up against' such an eminent expert. Astoundingly, although this would have been bad enough, the doctor had then added that if he was forced to provide evidence he would have to agree with finding of abuse so he would not contradict his respected colleague.

It becomes blindingly obvious that our solicitor is unable to find doctors to answer the three-page list of questions that we and the barrister have drafted. Without their help we are unable to place the whole stack of medical anomalies and relevant facts before the court. Should we instruct another solicitor so late in the day? We could find our own experts but we have no funds to pay them. How can we win against a system that lets medical opinion be provided by a select few experts, whom others fail to question?

What would the general public make of a secretive system that can snipe at parents from the safety of the court, without redress or reason? Darron and I want to take our children home, free from the input of those claiming to know better than us as parents. Losing suddenly seems inevitable, without the help of those we have trusted to represent us. The suitcases of evidence, documents and medical research stand firmly zipped shut and all the judge will see is the accusation of a doctor, who will have long since moved on to the next case and banked the payment.

Prior to the next court hearing, Marie telephones us to query a suggestion put forward by our solicitor, Julie. It emerges that, whilst attending a professionals meeting with the Guardian and the three legal teams connected to the case, our legal representatives had taken it upon themselves to offer a deal to the Local Authority in order to try and secure our return home.

Marie had been surprised by the revelation that we had offered to have CCTV installed in our home to provide full monitoring of us with our children. I was as astounded as Marie had been, to discover that our solicitor had stated that we would be prepared to film our every move and that we consented to the footage being reviewed by the other parties involved.

Fortunately the Local Authority solicitor and the Guardian's had expressed the view that CCTV would not be appropriate and would infringe on our rights. Darron and I were left astounded and appalled that our legal team had acted without any instruction from us and that they were prepared to offer outlandish arrangements, without any consultation with us, their clients.

In early spring of 2005 our legal team starts to add to the pressure we are under. I have been warned in my conversations with Rioch of the 'Five Percenters' support group, that often solicitors will follow procedural lines and fail to give attention to important factors in complicated cases. Darron and I again discuss the option of changing our legal team but it will be time consuming and we have no idea if another solicitor will be more likely to fight on our behalf.

Our solicitor's initial joy at taking on a case without evidence had been undermined by their willingness to let the Local Authority fish around for a more damning and definitive report and now that they would have to work to protect us, they were losing interest. For years after the case ended, I would read articles and blogs from parents, who would say the same. Finding the right solicitor was more luck than judgment.

It was on one of the many forays into the high court that had now become so familiar to us, as we sat in the café awaiting the start of the hearing, that our solicitor and barrister came to talk to us. We had long since grown used to the fact that often we would hardly see our legal team, as they had taken on a new case that involved the local authority's barrister and they would now invariably be found in a huddle on the opposite side of the coffee shop.

The scene had become such a regular event that, on numerable occasions, the only other person left feeling abandoned was the social worker. It became almost routine that if we saw each other we would sit together in a threesome, her telling us we shouldn't be there and us nodding without further comment, before launching into the latest antics or newly developed skills of Mark or Sean.

It seemed to us that there were only three people in the system that were actually interested in the welfare of the children in the case and they were all sat together, watching the legal representatives talk shop. Of course I have no idea if some of those conversations included our case. I'm sure, from some of the wry smiles, that deals were being offered or struck and it became obvious that discussions had taken place when, that day, the barrister asks to hold a private discussion in one of the meeting rooms.

The meeting room is little more than a large changing cubicle with a table and we gather round it to hear what our legal representative has to say. The offer is simple; if we sign the 'threshold document' we will be able to go home. If we sign one piece of paper the final hearing can be scheduled within weeks and we can end the legal battle once and for all. The only problem is that we have no idea what a threshold document is.

We would later be told that we should never have signed the document under any guise. Nobody though would forgive us for wanting to sign anything that meant the agreed safe return of our children to our sole care and the promise of a life free to do whatever we pleased.

We are lectured on the unfairness of a causation hearing and the inevitable outcome that one of us would be accused of shaking Sean. The barrister asks me if our relationship will stand the stress of one of us being labeled forever as an abuser. As Darron talks to our solicitor the barrister leans into me and asks if I think my husband would cope if he was the one named. We both knew he wouldn't.

The Local Authority, from our perspective, seem to be offering a plea bargain. Marie would inform us later that she knew of no such insinuation but we both hear the offer. Sign the paperwork, attend the final hearing and go home. The sticking point being that the 'threshold' would mean admitting to abusing our son. Darron and I both refuse point blank. How could we look our son in the eye in the future and tell me him that we had agreed to abusing him? No way. It would never happen. The barrister leaves the room and

Darron and I share a look of disbelief. How could we have come so far and then be led to this?

Social Services had investigated our family, they had made or arranged over three hundred visits by professionals and plagued us in the early days of the case with phone calls and threats, yet they had never raised one concern over either our parenting or the welfare of the children. In fact, all the assessments of us were remarkably favourable, referring constantly to our emotional warmth, loving and caring attitudes and excellent standards of care.

It seems that there is only one reason we are in court proceedings and that is simply because we can't offer an alternative explanation to a medical finding, on a scan that an eminent doctor had spent years learning to interpret. The eminence was obviously more important than the relevance, as no other medical specialist had been called for. Sean's medical notes are off limits to us and so we never see the scan. How could we dispute the 'facts' as we were given them? How could we defend against an accusation so all encompassing, other than to stand our ground and state we would never injure our children?

We had played ball, we had moved out of our own home and we had endured hours of visits, some lasting most of the day. We had been put under immense pressure and had 'failed to crack', why now would we confess? I suppose, though, if you put enough pressure on anyone for long enough, they will all crack in the end. Confession gained, case proven, statistic recorded.

Darron and I discuss at length the possibility of signing a threshold agreement in order to expedite our return home and end what has become a very frustrating, stressful and exasperating case. We talk openly, going round in circles as we revisit the pros and cons of the decision and come back each time to the fact that neither of us can bring ourselves to admit a false acceptance of guilt for Sean's injury. Kate, our barrister, was now weary of trying to persuade us to 'help ourselves' by shortening the court battle, thereby making life easier on everyone.

In a final bid to shake our nerve we are given all the possible outcomes of a causation hearing, including the possibility that one of us will never be able to have access to our children, if we are found to have committed the alleged offence. I feel myself go back to that time when we had been told by Mary Howard that any confession would be better than none. I listen to the circular argument that, without admission of guilt, the judge won't be able to allow us home, as the risk will be too great, whilst I wonder how a 'confessed guilty parent' will be allowed home either.

We are now facing what feels like a sub-trial by our own legal team as they 'sell' to us our best chance at living a normal life with our children. There is no way in a million years Darron and I can admit falsely to injuring our son and the argument comes to an abrupt halt when a compromise is offered. If the medical evidence is such that an injury has occurred, including the possibility raised by other medical professionals that the timing included Sean's time in hospital, could we concede that in that instance we had failed to protect Sean from the injury?

In all the years we have been married, never has a decision been so hard to make. We call my parents, speak to friends and discuss the proposition that we, as parents, had failed our young son in not preventing what had happened.

We still firmly believe that the cause is medical but we have no doctor prepared to back up our belief, just plenty of past cases, strange anomalies, issues with Sean's medical care and anecdotal evidence. Whichever way we look at it, it is less of a leap to admit to failing him than it is to admit to abusing him.

We eventually consent with one condition, we insist that the threshold document carries a caveat that should a medical cause is found we can return to court.

The barrister words and re-words what became known as the 'preamble', mainly because that's what the judge referred to it as. It is important to us that the preamble is the first part of the document that anyone in the future will read; we want to shout, for all to hear, that we, as parents, brow beaten and weary, have not forsaken our child. That in the case of Sean's injuries we will stand before the world, stating that we have only failed to protect him, whilst the cause is alleged to have been deliberate.

We need to know that if a medical cause was found, all bets were off and we stated that we were prepared to pick up the gauntlet again and redress the one-sided argument that had got us where we presently stood. It gave us a chance that one day we might be able to fight to clear our names.

My hand shakes, the tremor noticeable, as I sign the agreement, praying that Sean will forgive me if I have let him down and praying that my belief that an answer will one day be found, will be proved true in my lifetime. The room is warm and the air stuffy, but I shiver, the knowledge that it is a final decision making me immediately unsure. I cannot turn back the clock, I can only go forward and I swear that I will do all I can as a mother to prove my worth. It is December 2004 and we are going home for Christmas.

It only strikes me as odd later, in the cold light of day, that at no point did our legal team offer to even try and fight the accusation. They never mentioned the medical witnesses we had specifically asked for, the inference was that the medical reports that had been provided to the court were from very eminent experts in their field and it would be hard to persuade any other specialists to counter their claims. I wonder how they knew if they never tried? Nearly five years after our final hearing, two of the eminent doctors would fall from grace but that was in the future and today they were still eminent.

The threshold agreement signed, we go before the judge. To this day I have no memory of that hearing; apart from a discussion as to the merits of instructing a clinical psychologist to assess Darron and myself. The Guardian, Isaac, is insistent that a report is submitted before he makes any recommendations to the court. I have no issue with any psychological assessment any more than Darron does. We have no reason to hide anything and we will do anything to end this nightmare.

The Local Authority feels there is nothing to be gained from the assessment other than information that has already been obtained from the investigation of Social Services. In the end, the judge directs that the psychologist be instructed as soon as possible so as not to hold up the case. Marie O'Dwyer questions the usefulness of a report as she herself has a background in psychology and has spent a massive amount of time with us.

Her opinion is not in any way to deflect from the plethora of academic achievements of the psychologist instructed or his expertise in his field, merely that one meeting, no matter how well constructed, would not be able to add further evidence to the court. Put like that we can only agree.

In the end the delay is considerable. The final hearing that is booked for December is postponed as the psychologist has still not been able to find time to meet with us and the alternative psychologists suggested do not meet with the Guardians approval. Spring approaches and we are yet again playing a waiting game.

The children's names are removed from the 'at risk' register on the 13th April 2005, prior to receipt of the psychologist's report. The case conference concludes that there were never any concerns raised about us as parents or about the children's welfare during the entire time of their involvement. We are now in the remarkable situation of going to a final hearing with both children no longer classed as 'at risk'.

Darron and I don't care. The constant adverts on the television from the NSPCC goad us whenever we see them. Their statistics of children at risk include children like ours; children whose parents have never done anything except fail to explain an injury, that is later attributed to something medical. Even now, if we see that statistic, we both glower at the screen. Our children have never been at risk from us, only from those who failed to investigate anything other than suppositions and accusations.

CHAPTER 24.

The Clinical Psychologist's report is dated 27th April 2005. Dr. Michael Hoskins, previously employed as a senior psychologist for Barnardo's, consultant to several fostering and adoption agencies and author of, in his own words, 'numerous articles and journals' and a book on counselling and psychotherapy, arranges a meeting at our home to take place without the children present.

It is interesting to note that, following his long and detailed list of qualifications and the background of the case, that he has been provided with, his very first observations were to record that we were co-operative but that we had resisted the initial meeting date *he* had requested. I distinctly remember the conversation on the phone, following introductions, where he set out a visit date and time that was at short notice and difficult to arrange childcare for, being a Sunday. Although we would never have wished for the children to be with anyone other than ourselves, the professionals involved in the case often failed to take account that, for us, we had to work to pay our mortgage, regardless of whether we were living at our home, we had to feed and clothe our children and we would have to arrange childcare.

In response to arranging another date I am advised that the date he has suggested and chosen, is his own child's birthday and he will have to sacrifice the occasion to meet with us. He had, he informed me, a very hectic and busy schedule. His report notes; "There was some initial resistance to meeting with the appointment I suggested, although this was overcome with explanation and persistence". The report hadn't even begun and he was already giving a negative impression of us. He fails to document at this point that, despite living an hour and half away from our house, he arrives two hours late! I can't help but wonder how many psychologists would still see you if you were two hours late for an appointment. Perhaps we should have given him marks for his 'persistence!'

Upon arriving and having been made the customary hot drink he immediately sits down on the sofa opposite the television. I smile to myself, wondering if this ruse to pick the most used chair in the house is to 'unsettle' us. I have read books about psychology and my knowledge is amateur in the extreme but I decide it probably is. Game on, I think to myself and I believe that's all it is to him, a game to see which one of us 'trips up' first, which one 'cracks', which one shows any sign of anything other than normality.

It seems as if we are back in the early days, back when everything relied on opinion without fact. As I sit down in the chair opposite, Dr. Hoskins sets out his papers across the sofa and all I can think is; here we go again. He speaks to both of us together to advise us that whilst one of us is talking to him, the other must fill out some psychometric questionnaires. He speaks with authority but in a calm tone as he asks Darron to go first and takes him into the kitchen to explain the test.

I notice that it has stopped raining and my thoughts drift back to my children, who have been waiting at great grandma's now for three hours. I know they are safe and I know that they are happy, oblivious to the events that are going on around them. Keep calm I instruct myself and tell the truth - whatever he asks, answer it.

My thoughts are interrupted by a summoning call from the kitchen. Darron looks over to me with a frustrated look on his face. It is not one he uses often, he is an intuitive being and generally acts as he feels; of the two of us I am more cautious. I look up at Dr. Hoskins, who shows no kind of readable expression, as he asks: "What is the answer to this sample question?" I have no idea now what the question was, it is a lifestyle choice question, what would you do if…? I read through the question and look at the multiple choice answers. Using gut instinct, I answer 'B.'

While he looks from one of us to the other he dismissively passes the rest of the question paper to Darron and asks that he completes it in private and away from the living room. I later find out that having spoken to Darron like a complete moron, Dr. Hoskins had explained that there was no right or wrong answer to the question. He then proceeded to tell Darron that he had got the question wrong. I ask him which answer he had chosen and he grins; "I answered 'B' too." Oh dear, things are not looking great.

As I sit with the psychologist I recall the events of the last eighteen months. The report records my feelings that the hospital doctors' questions were ambiguous; the reason for their inquiries only becoming obvious after Social Services got involved. The paper records in black and white my statement that, whatever we said, was never enough.

Dr. Hoskins makes repeated reference to how the injuries have been identified as non-accidental, possibly attributed to shaking, and he asks me to explain the injury. I tell him all I know, that it was a subdural bleed and that Sean had been born early. I state that I would never injure Sean and Darron would never injure Sean. I try my best to put him in the picture. We have been honest with family and friends and we have not hidden what is going on from them, we have been honest to ourselves and we still feel the cause is a medical one.

The psychologist would eventually conclude, in a document written single-sided over several pages, how I was "steadfast in my belief" that there was a medical cause for Sean's injury. I didn't need a report to tell me that, we never wavered, we were sure. There are a large number of pages in the report relating to things that have happened in my life and Dr. Hoskins concludes at one point that I am too forgiving.

He suggests this to me, when he interviews me and I try to explain that I was brought up a Catholic; I attend church and try to lead a good life. I know I am not perfect and I don't expect perfection in others. I have always tried to forgive when necessary and help where I can, that is my nature. Some might voice the opinion that I get 'used' but I know what I am doing and I am not foolish. If we do not look after the other people in our lives, what is life for?

I consider the possibility that his opinion, that I should be angry or resent the things that have happened in my life, is more of an indication of his own character than mine. After everything I have endured, it is a good job that I can still see people as people, flaws and all, and, if necessary, forgive. Dr. Hoskins questions further some of my beliefs and views, at one point stating that I am incorrect in my analysis of a situation, based on the fact that it reflects family beliefs and not 'macro social perspective'. I still have no idea what that means, I say what I believe and I don't expect others to agree.

In asking me why I was interested in dating Darron I reply honestly that his sense of humour and honesty attracted me. I like the fact that like a lot of people from the Midlands I have met, he speaks his mind. As the doctor continues his cross-examination, he asks why we undertook a long distance relationship (Darron was working in Birmingham, living in Swadlincote, and I was studying in Nottingham and living in Buxton). I knew at the time people thought it wouldn't last but fifteen years on, here we are. It just felt right.

The psychologist analyses my choice to study engineering and my loss of a career in that industry after the birth of Mark. He suggests to me that, having been a woman with knowledge and a career, I must have struggled 'giving it up' to have children. I reply that I couldn't go back to my old job, as I had been told that I couldn't offer the level of commitment required now I had a family. Did I want to go back anyway? I'm not sure.

I used to work long hours and I did not have a child to place him in childcare. I looked for a part-time job near to home and got a job in a local pharmacy. The in-house training was interesting and the work varied. I still had plenty of time to take Mark swimming, to playgroups and to see friends. I don't think I ever felt a 'gap' in my life, other than the desire for a second child.

He presses on, asking whether or not Darron coped with being a father. I reply that he is a good dad, he was like most men, quite unsure at first, uncertain and nervous. Dr. Hoskins questions whether or not our relationship as a couple has changed, to which I reply; "Intensely, it moves you to a different plane with new opportunities and it kills off opportunities. You can't compare them but it is not worse, just different."

The scrutiny of our relationship doesn't end there. I am asked to explain why I chose to marry a non-graduate, instead of someone with the same level of education. I reply that I like down-to-earth men. I am not interested in a man, who wants to be a high flier, to get to a certain place. I study to learn and master the topic, not for advancement. I inform him that Darron is very intelligent man who lacked opportunity for advancement but not the ability.

He argues that I am the more dominant one and that I have chosen a lower qualified man in order to assert this perceived dominance. His insistence, easily perceptible in his report, states that he believes this to be the case but he writes that I may wish to argue otherwise. Too right I do! I suspect that personal opinions of the evaluator are key to his conclusion.

It is worthy of note that many times Dr. Hoskins mentions Darron's lack of qualifications, despite the fact that he served an apprenticeship, holds several NVQ's at A-level standard and has an Advanced City and Guilds qualifications and additional qualifications gained through his work. It would seem to me that in the case of the psychologist, unless the qualification adds letters after your name, it isn't a recognised qualification.

It would be interesting to know what happens in his house when the roof leaks, a new boiler needs fitting or the electricity supply needs upgrading. We all have our strengths and I would guess that unless he was going to fill a hole in the roof with the journals and articles he has written, he would be unable to fix the problem himself. His constant insistence that my university education means that I somehow married beneath me is the kind of closed thinking that leads some professionals to state opinions as fact and their cohorts to defer to them.

When finally I am asked about the effects of the visiting professionals, I tell him the truth, they are invasive and it is extremely stressful. There is immense pressure to make up incidents to fit the injury, to act a certain way, to fit in with the timetable the social worker has arranged for us and the added burden of the financial cost of court visits and childcare whilst the hearings take place. We are financially struggling as Darron is still missing shift payments for days he is off work, attending meetings and court hearings. Childcare costs are constant factor in trying to meet with Social Services and court requirements, the offer of help made and then retracted.

CHAPTER 25.

As we waited for the report, Social Services had again decided to offer childcare for Sean paid for by the Local Authority and the decision to take up the offer is not ours to make. We are told that we must no longer allow Wendy, the childminder, who has become a close friend of the family since Mark's birth, to care for the children and must instead find a nursery to provide the childcare. The reason for this becomes quickly apparent as I am informed that the staff will be expected to write reports on the children's progress, development and welfare.

Social Services stipulate that the care must take place on the days and at the times specified and it does not escape my notice that the dates seem to fall overwhelmingly when Darron usually cares for the children at home. Our children will now be in childcare much more often than either of us are happy with and we firmly believe that the ground rules will change almost as soon as they are agreed.

The final hearing is supposed to be taking place in a matter of weeks, as soon as the psychologists report is in. We both voice the opinion that, as soon as the ink on the nursery reports is dry, funding will stop. Darron asks Marie if payment for the childcare will be withdrawn suddenly, as there is no way we can meet the costs of a nursery place for both children at short notice, he is reassured repeatedly that this will not be the case. The daily increase in their combined childcare would be far more than it had been with the childminder and although we have had no say in the decision, we will have to pay for Mark's place as Social Services advise us there is no more funding.

While Darron and Marie go to meet the manager of the nursery and arrange for two trial sessions for both children, I am so upset that I can't bring myself to go. I am frustrated that I can no longer send Mark to Wendy, the childminder who has been looking after him for the last two years. Wendy feeds Mark and Sean the food I cook and fills me in on their day in great detail. Mark plays endlessly with her own daughter, who is the same age and he is always excited when he sees her.

Sean would be with a larger group of children at a nursery and I loathe the arrangement, preferring the boys to be with one carer than with a number of different nursery nurses. I suspect that, yet again, the system will provide with one hand and take away with the other.

The following week I get the children ready in the morning and take them the short distance to the only nursery in the village. I know that a number of mums have chosen it as the best place to provide care for their children and there is no reason why I should feel anxious, I just can't shake the feeling.

The building is bright and light and adorned with all kinds of popular children's characters. The staff seem welcoming and easy to spot in their matching blue polo shirts with the nursery's logo on. I for my part, feel self-conscious as I know that the manager has already spoken with the social worker and I believe I will be judged. I am not naïve enough to think that the staff are completely unaware of the circumstances and I am sure that some staff will think there is 'no smoke without fire'.

The noise is overwhelming as there are so many children with four different age groups in one open plan area. The babies are kept in a partitioned space, with a baby gate, in order to keep them safe and to prevent the older children from hurting them during the inevitable rough and tumble. The provision looks great, with lots of different activities on offer: - painting, drawing, building blocks, sand, water and reading books. There is everything a child could want to play with but the staff are exceptionally busy.

Wendy has always baked with the children, painted, taken them to toddler groups and arranged quiet time to read and rest. Here everything happens simultaneously, with children moving from one activity to the next, without cohesion or thought. There is nothing wrong with any of it except that it isn't what I want for my children. I hug and kiss them goodbye and leave uncertainly. I have briefly met the key workers, a different one for Mark and Sean due to their ages, but I barely have time to introduce myself as other parents jostle to leave instructions and advice with regard to their own children.

I walk to work drained. The children will be well cared for I am sure, yet I simply want to return to life before we had to meet demands or consult third parties. We have been left with the care of our children but we don't have free say in the choices that are made. We will be paying for Mark's place even though we would rather he was somewhere else and Darron and I have discussed at length what we will do when Sean's place is no longer funded. We still feel Sean's place will only be paid for up until the time that the reports are in, after that we are sure we will be abandoned to try and meet the extra childcare costs that will inevitably follow or risk having to resettle our two children again.

I have only been at work for an hour and a half when the phone rings. I think nothing of it as I continue to put on my coat in order to pick up the latest batch of prescriptions from the doctors surgery nearby. Sandra, my co-worker, answers the call and I hear the tap of the receiver on the work surface as she places it down, calling my name. As I get to the phone I look at her quizzically and she responds by saying; "It's the nursery, they are asking for you."

Immediately my heart quickens, what has happened? Is it Sean? He had been well when I left him but perhaps he has been fretful in his new surroundings. I pick up the phone in a bid to get answers to the questions whizzing around my head. Even I don't anticipate what comes next. "Mr. Toomey has taken Mark to the hospital. He has suffered a head injury following an incident with another boy." I can't even imagine what kind of incident they are referring to but I don't care. My initial reaction is one of worry and disbelief and then, as I hang up the phone, anger. It seems that every time Social Services make some request or demand under the guise of helping our family we end up picking up the pieces.

"How is Mark? How bad is the injury?" I talk to my colleagues as I fetch my mobile and dial Darron's number, which unsurprisingly goes straight to the answer phone. The only consolation I reason - is that, if they have waited for Darron to come and fetch Mark he mustn't be seriously injured. I can't do anything more except wait and worry and I am so used to the constant knot in my stomach it barely makes any difference. I serve more customers and my friends try to comfort me as I wait for more news, unsure as to the location of my husband and son.

Nearly an hour after the call from the nursery and after several more calls from customers, the phone rings again and it is Darron calling. As I answer with the pharmacy's name and standard greeting he interrupts, instantly recognizing my voice. "It's me. We are still at the hospital but we are leaving shortly, the doctor and nurses have just glued Mark's head back together. They have said that it will most likely scar but that due to the way he was injured and the depth of the injury, they are unable to stitch it or use those strip things. We should be back by the time you go for lunch and I can pick you up if you like."

Aggravated by the fact that I have been unable to be there for Mark and upset at the fact that he has been injured at all, I agree and replace the phone on its' cradle on the wall, before simply looking at my boss and shaking my head in disbelief. It has been so long since I have cried over anything that I no longer feel connected to my own emotions anymore and the only thing that will make me feel any better is to see Mark for myself.

When the car pulls up outside work I climb into the passenger seat and immediately turn around. Mark looks at me and smiles as I take in the bruises that are already appearing near his eyes. In the middle of his eyebrows, just above the bridge of his nose there is a gauze pad tapped in place with micropore. I turn back as I put my seat belt on and Darron simply adds, "What an absolute cock up!" I glance over at him as he sets off for the short drive home and I ask: "For Heaven's sake what happened?"

Darron fills me in on all he knows, which is a little sketchy due to the speed at which Mark required treatment. It seemed apparent that another boy had taken a dislike to Mark as a newcomer and had pushed him headlong into the end of a metal radiator, which left unprotected, had been driven into Mark's forehead.

Once we are home I ring Marie at Social Services to advise her of what has happened and she immediately adopts an apologetic tone, as she expresses concern about the incident. There is nothing any of us can do about the injury now - there is no point in trying to apportion blame, although as the conversation continues it transpires others fear being held responsible for the injury. The nursery contacted Marie's office only a short time after Mark had been taken to hospital and reported that the child, who had pushed Mark in a fit of pique, was known to be aggressive towards smaller children and three other parents had already complained.

That fact did little to dispel my worries about having to send Mark back to nursery, now knowing that they had been aware of a possible situation and had not protected my son, who was significantly younger and smaller that the other child, from his extreme dislike. It seemed that my children were more at risk from the system than anything else, as every decision made without our consent for their supposed wellbeing did more harm than good.

I kept my manner calm and friendly on the phone to Marie, knowing that she had no part in the events that had occurred but inside I was seething. My feelings had no bearing on the decisions being made and I sensed that voicing my concerns was futile. We would be left trying to reassure Mark, whose bruises were darkening by the minute and, despite our misgivings, we would still expected to ensure that both Sean and Mark attended the nursery the following day.

Eventually the nursery became more familiar to all of us as the staff tried hard to settle the children, following the traumatic start Mark had experienced. I find myself thinking back intermittently, considering how much I miss the information that used to be provided by Wendy about the children's day and the homeliness that is lacking from the busy environment that the nursery provides but, in truth, mostly it becomes just a routine.

There are times when I feel aggrieved that the decision was ever taken, particularly when we have family photographs taken and the scar is clearly visible upon Mark's forehead. I am aware of it even today, when nearly eight years on, faded, whiter and yet still noticeable, it stands as a marker of everything that happened to us and how wrong it all was.

Only a couple of months after the stipulation of nursery care had been put in place and with our childminder having filled the places, we were proved right again. Social Services retract the funding of Sean's place and leave us with only a few days notice to find the extra money for that month's nursery bill. It is a massive strain and Marie is left apologising profusely, clearly unaware of the intention to remove funding so quickly.

Darron telephones the manager at Social Services and asks incredulously, why they have done the very thing they promised they would not do. The answer he is given is impassive: We need to prove we can cope alone as parents

---

188

before the final hearing. I exclaim to Darron in disbelief that, if that is what they wanted, they shouldn't have got so involved in the first place. Of course the real answer to why there is no longer funding available is that the funding was only ever provided so that Social Services could ask for reports to be written. Darron and I always assumed, once the paperwork was completed, that would be the end of the matter.

Looking back I can see that reports of happy, cheerful, friendly children, written by trained nursery nurses, ultimately only helped our case but it didn't escape our notice that a nursery nurse changing nappies and toileting a toddler would be perfectly placed to check for any bruises or injuries. The irony of course being, the only injury that had ever occurred in all the boys time at nursery, took place whilst our children were in their care.

CHAPTER 26.

Some weeks after the nursery incident had been confined to the case log book, Marie O'Dwyer rings me to advise me that Dr. Hoskins' report is in. This is a huge piece of news as not only are we waiting to see if he will support the children staying with us but it also means the wait is over and we can go to the final hearing. She brings a copy of the report with her that afternoon and leaves it with me to read. The document, forty one pages in length, covers the aspects which we have talked about and his interpretation of the psychometric tests he performed.

Dr. Hoskins records what I have said in such a way that it appears, at first glance, to be almost verbatim, yet upon reading it, I quickly notice that some of what I said has been misconstrued and parts left out. The small nuances that allow you to get the bigger picture are replaced with childish connectives. As far as I know I have never spoken in clipped, short staccato like tones but you would be forgiven for thinking so upon reading the report. The only relevant 'significant scores' he can find on my tests are for 'The Demandingness Scale' and 'Role Restriction' I re-read the page several times trying to understand what is meant.

I am informed by the report that the scale refers to the pressures the child places on the parent. Dr. Hoskins is kind enough to write that this could be due to the care proceedings and medical problems Sean has had but the scale, he advises, is not meant to assess external factors, only direct demands of the child. It may have been prudent to make that clear on the tests but they are deliberately vague, designed to make you assess the meaning for yourself.

He also finds a significant score in relation to 'Role Restriction' and writes that this score is due to parents seeing themselves being controlled and dominated by their child's demands and needs. It doesn't take a psychology degree to work out that you might be a little angry and 'constrained' by monitoring, visits and the need to live away from home like nomads for such a considerable length of time.

I go onto read about Darron's meeting and his test scores. The first thing I see is that he has spelt Darren in the traditional sense. Despite the fact that the spelling is unusual (his mother would insist unique and interesting) you would assume that a doctor writing about a patient would at least be able to correctly spell their name! I sigh in resignation but read on.

The details of Darron's interview are similar, after all they reflect the same views, we both believe Sean's injury has a medical cause. Darron confirms that, in his opinion, neither one of us is dominant in our relationship, (Darron would joke today, more is the pity). I have to say from my perspective, the experiences we have been through have made us both less trusting of others. I no longer tolerate untruths, as I once did and I won't put up with injustice. I am a stronger person because of it all.

As I continue to turn the pages, it becomes clear who the psychologist believes is the likely perpetrator of the injury. The sentences constantly enforce the view that although Darron has not said anything directly to raise an issue, there is a definite need for observation. There is a distinct undertone in the words and the way they are phrased but he states clearly that it would be "too simplistic and unacceptable to identify him [Darron] as the likely perpetrator". Surely though, in writing that very phrase, he is suggesting the very same thing?

Dr. Hoskins can find no indication of elevated scores on the tests and attributes this to the possibility of Darron 'faking good' on a test that supposedly can't be faked. He implies that an average test score is not a true reflection, despite the word "average" inferring that most peoples' scores would fall in the same range.

By page thirty nine, Dr. Hoskins finally attempts to return to his remit and answer the questions that were initially asked of him by the court. His first line of paragraph one states that, "The mother accepts that an N.A.I. happened, but cannot identify the perpetrator." This was never the case and his own report mentions my steadfast opinion that neither of us could or would injure Sean. By paragraph two he contradicts both Darron's and my opinion that we share in an equal relationship. Dr. Hoskins knowing better after only an hour, equivocally states that I am more dominant. In reaction to the fact that this is against the testimony of both us and the social worker he adds that he takes the view that I am "sufficiently skilful in manipulation" and that the "equal balance of power within our relationship is a façade".

How clever am I? Even I didn't know how manipulating I could be. So in spite of the fact that not several pages before I have also been portrayed as an overly forgiving person who was at risk of being taken advantage of, as a person who was, "Warm, sympathetic and supportive", I am also apparently domineering and manipulative.

The report continues with Dr. Hoskins' belief that our past history of working with the Local Authority would mean we would continue to work constructively and continue to attend appointments. He states it would be difficult to assess one or other of us as the perpetrator of the injury, contradicting his previous insinuation and suggesting instead that we are in denial. He recommends the Local Authority's continual involvement as there is "no clear indication of anger impulse control difficulties in either parent or violent behaviour." It seems that the danger comes from neither of us being assessed as being a danger.

In his final conclusion, after forty pages of writing and self-contradiction, Dr. Hoskins ends a lengthy and wordy report stating that in his view a supervision order would not be appropriate due to the seriousness of the injuries. He questions whether police checks have been carried out and requests access to all our medical reports. After nearly eighteen months of investigations Dr Hoskins' final blow is to ask for a separate investigation in relation to Mark and any historical injuries he may have sustained.

I flick back over the document in my hand. My first thought is how, after one meeting, our lives and personalities are determined by the answers we gave, the tests we took, but more importantly by the disclosure that Sean was injured. The instruction that we would later receive through our solicitors confirms that Dr. Hoskins fee will be paid by all parties in equal measure. I am reminded a little of the crucifixion. In child abuse cases it seems you must carry your own cross.

In respect of Dr. Hoskins, I am sure his years working as a clinical psychologist have allowed him to see past the obvious, sometimes a little too much so. In order to determine the likely perpetrator you must first believe there is a perpetrator. With the previous experts in the case writing reports stating as much, there is no room to doubt the 'evidence'. Little remains except to ascertain blame. It becomes merely a case of the person with the likeliest motive or opportunity.

In reference to the interviews Dr. Hoskins carried out, he was always working upon the assumption that one of us was guilty. If we expressed the opinion that the bleed in Sean's brain could be due to a medical cause, we were portrayed as delusional and in denial.

From the high ground it is easy to pull apart a person's life, to cast aspersions and lay blame. I am struck by how hard it is to determine the meaning of the deliberately ambiguous and sometimes down-right misleading questions. You have in the back of your mind your children and what you are going through. As truthfully as I answered, I couldn't be sure I answered the questions accurately.

If I, as in Dr. Hoskins most knowledgeable opinion, a university graduate, a qualified person, struggled to understand and comprehend, how are parents who have not had the family support or opportunities I had, expected to cope? Is the system prepared to assess likely guilt of a parent on the answers of those same parents who may struggle to ascertain the meaning of the question?

It may seem that I have a particular dislike of clinical psychology but I don't. I believe it can be enlightening, it can provide a piece of a puzzle. However, is it fair that after eighteen months of threats and continued daily pressure any credence at all is given to the mental state of either Darron or myself at the time of Sean's admission? If you keep trying to break something until it breaks, you can't complain it is broken. If you take a family and tear them apart, you cannot then determine with any certainty whether the family could function before or can function after.

CHAPTER 27.

The weeks following the psychologist's opinion were reserved for the legal teams to draft their cases. Social Services had never put much store on the need for psychological assessment, preferring instead to base their opinions on extensive and often intrusive monitoring. Whatever we feel about the intrusions at least we can say that we have demonstrated good parenting and the ability to cope well under pressure.

The Guardian also makes a trip to meet with us for the first time at our family home. He remarks on the noticeable difference in the surroundings as the children, now more relaxed and happy, play in the garden. The final hearing has been moved several times due to the delay in obtaining Dr. Hoskins' report, but it is eventually scheduled again for start of June and we are all gearing up for our last days in court.

By now we have been to a whole list of courts: Chesterfield Magistrates Court, Derby County Court, Bolton Combined Court, Manchester High Court and the High Court in London. Darron and I have a particularly stressful weekend arranging transport for one of the court hearings in London, having only been told of the change late on a Friday. Having never really travelled to the capital, Darron books a very expensive train ticket and arrives in London only to be greeted by delay after delay.

He later discovers that there has been a major rally blocking half the streets and he struggles to find his way by tube and eventually taxi. The venue has been dictated by the Local Authority barrister, who apparently was unable to make the hearing in Manchester due to other commitments. The hearing is adjourned because of a problem with paperwork for the second time, rendering the trip useless.

Compellingly, we are never allowed to make such demands with regard to times, dates or venues, another example of how the system leans towards the professionals and away from the parents, whose travel expenses are not paid and who have had to seek time off work to attend.

The final hearing has so long been our target that we have never considered what might actually happen when it takes place. The long and protracted arguments about the merits of certain 'experts' and the need for all sides to hold views so diametrically opposed is past. Darron and I chat to the Guardian about his new found love of motorbikes, having been enthusiastic riders ourselves.

We mention some of the more famous Derbyshire runs that are so often frequented by bikers and the pubs that offer a welcome drink and a meal, without you feeling out of place dressed head to toe in leather. Darron and I had once been amazed when we had visited a local country pub in the middle of nowhere and had been shown to a beautiful dining room.

The excellent service and beautiful food was only beaten by the value for money and we resolved that we would visit the pub again with a view to making it a more regular occurrence. We reviewed our opinions when we arrived on our motorbike, dressed in leathers, and were shown to the smallest, most cramped table for two in the smokey bar. It seems that even in a tiny country pub, six miles from the nearest town, there is a dress code!

Obviously the other regular attendee at court was our social worker, Marie. Marie had long since snubbed the company of the Derbyshire legal team and had taken to joining us in a pre-hearing tea and a chat. The mood was always much stiffer than in our lounge at home, but friendly nonetheless. We would talk about wider topics as the children were not present, discussing travel and history and often telling her of our desire to take the children to visit Santa in Lapland.

By the final hearing we had taken to discussing various cases where people had been wrongly accused or convicted and the work of the author and humanist campaigner, Ludovic Kennedy. Kennedy had questioned the safety of the convictions of several high profile murderers and his book "Miscarriages of Justice" detailed the case of Timothy Evans, who was hanged for the murder of his wife and baby daughter. The convicted man, with the help of Kennedy's revelations, was posthumously pardoned as the real murderer confessed to both murders and those of a further five victims.

The public outrage that arose from the realisation that a man had gone to the gallows and died an innocent man helped abolish the death penalty in the UK. The three of us would exclaim disbelief that men and women could be hanged on evidence that was so flawed. These sorts of miscarriages of justice are fortunately rare but show that evidence can't be used if it is not available. There will always be cases where the most likely explanation is not the correct one. There were several cases of mothers accused of murdering their babies on the basis of the statistics provided by, a then eminent, expert. The expert, who stated at the time, "One sudden infant death is a tragedy, two is suspicious and three is murder, until proved otherwise" was widely believed and used as a witness by the police and Social Services.

Further scientific research eventually challenged the theory and led to a judicial review of a number of high profile cases. If we fail to question those whose opinion is informed by statistical likelihood, without the consideration of other factors, we risk conviction on the basis of nothing more than a betting system, based on statistical analysis rather than proof.

Marie, Darron and I finish our drinks and smile wanly at each other as we go to join our respective legal teams. We file into the court room in Preston High Court with one last battle to face. The Local Authority, contrary to what they had led us to believe, have decided at the last minute to apply for a supervision order; an order that does not give the Authority parental responsibility but allows them a period of one year in which to continue to monitor and befriend the child.

The Guardian is also requesting that a supervision order be made in order to reflect the seriousness of Sean's injury and refers to Dr. Hoskins' opinion that an order is necessary. This is in direct contravention of the 'no order principle', which clearly states that if all parties are in agreement and co-operating there is no need for an order to be made.

Although the Guardian refers to Dr. Hoskins' report in requesting the order, the report itself had already been discarded by the judge at a previous hearing. We had all been present at court for a video conference with the presiding judge, a few weeks earlier, when she had declared, "I think we can all agree that Dr. Hoskins' has over stepped his remit." Wasn't that the understatement of a century? The judge had then slid the report to the end of her desk, indicating her lack of faith in it.

The Guardian's report for the court states that, as parents, we are both articulate and plausible and indicates that this may mean that Social Services could be 'taken in' by our account of what we believe happened. He fails to accept that we have proven ourselves repeatedly, his visits forming a tiny fraction of the visits we have been subjected to, instead, by inference, making out the other professionals are potentially gullible. The only other explanation for this plausible presentation might of course be that we are giving a valid and credible alternative explanation. Perhaps that thought should have been given more consideration and credence.

The judge listens to the Local Authority and Guardian's views and, as we have already heard our barrister's opinion that the judge will favour their requests, we sit as usual and listen. As intelligent people we know that the order will be made, our legal team has now resigned themselves to the fact and our barrister no longer feigns interest or demonstrates a willingness to fight, turning in court, shrugging her shoulders and mouthing the question; "What do you want me to say?"

What does she think she gets her wages for? We have had no medical findings or experts to answer the list of questions we have put together and so there is in effect no retort to the accusation. Yet again, we are herded into a room and told that it will 'look better' if we agree to the order rather than ask the judge to make the decision. Darron and I hold firm. Any impositions upon our family will be just that.

We know the judge will make the order, our barrister has brought no reference to any of the information we have provided her with, intending to let it happen and encouraging us to 'get it over with.' I refuse point blank to play ball anymore. I know the likely outcome and we have decided that the judge will make the decision so that Darron and I will never have to admit to our children that we accepted supervision was necessary.

As we leave the small meeting room and go back into court I see the court clerk and members of the Local Authority legal team hovering over the bench where we had been seated. I know why they are there. Determined that my sons will not be just another statistic, and sure that curiosity will get the better of those remaining in the court room whilst we are corralled in a side room, I have left a photograph on top of my papers.

The photo shows two happy, smiling faces, Mark with his arm around his brother as they grin at the camera. My sons are not a statistic, they are not a case and they are not a number. My children are individuals, they are people, and as their eyes shine brightly from the reflective paper I know that they will always be worth fighting for. I see that the photo has attracted attention and I note that people are discussing it.

Ultimately, as we file back in to court I project on them my thoughts - remember them. They are why you do your jobs, not for money or one-upmanship, not for glory, accolades or a step on the career ladder, but for children who really do need your help. But today, right here, right now my children are not they.

Soon after, the judge offers praise in the way we have conducted ourselves throughout and not detracting from the allegation of abuse, she appears kind and fair as she reads the documentary evidence of our parenting capacity, and smiling, recounts the record of the happy, bright children we have fought to protect.

The supervision order is made for a period of one year on the 14th June 2005. As she nods, wishing us well, I mouth "Thank you" knowing the court battle is over. Everyone in every direction shakes hands formally and Darron and I walk out into the summer sunshine with the end of our ordeal in sight.

CHAPTER 28.

The year passes remarkably quickly. The visits are perfunctory as there is no more assessing to be had. Sean impresses everyone he meets with his ability to entertain and amuse. By the age of three, Sean causes havoc whenever we are shopping by listening to the ring tones of passing people's mobile phones and waiting for them to hang up before mimicking them.

His ever friendly and loving manner is beguiling and telling him off without bursting into giggles is almost impossible. Sean hasn't a malicious bone in his body, everything he does he does with good intention even if his actions sometimes border on the annoyingly intense. Mark, more than anyone, is subjected to hero worship on an unprecedented scale and Sean cuddles him so often and so tightly that sometimes they both topple over, Mark unable to support Sean's weight. Mark, for his part, is the protective big brother, helping Sean in every way and teaching him concepts that Sean often fails to grasp but eagerly listens to all the same.

We put the house up for sale and, despite questions on where we are moving to, we keep the answer vague, only mentioning the town. We are not trying to be directly evasive, but we need to feel that our lives are our own again. The house we are living in we had intended to stay in whilst the children grew up, but it now feels somehow contaminated. So many people from the social workers, doctor, health visitor, nursery nurse, midwife, family support workers, psychologist, Guardian and solicitor all know our address and our home. It is no longer the sanctuary it once was and the memories we have are ones of miscarriages, sick children and legal battles.

Our neighbours beg us to stay, keen to convince us that we may move on from the way we feel and that the house might one day become a safe haven once again. On more than one occasion we reconsider, but we have both changed jobs. I have gone back into the world of IT and Darron has gone back to his roots in the building trade. We are rebuilding every part in our lives and a fresh start seems like the right thing to do.

It is nearly a year to the day from when the supervision order had been made that a letter drops on the doormat. I think nothing of it. The Derbyshire County Council logo is so familiar and letters have arrived so frequently for so long now, that I pay no real heed to the possible contents. The visits from Marie have been decreasing and life is starting to get back to what I suppose is normal as I tear open the envelope and read.

The letter is friendly and yet there is still an ever presence of professionalism. I realise that Marie had called the previous Tuesday and we had not been home. The visit wasn't a scheduled one and I had not been aware of her calling. Marie's letter mentions her leaving Social Services for personal reasons and she writes to wish our family well for the future.

It has been a considerable time since Marie and I have clashed over anything, since the orders inception there had been no more reasons to fight each other. We have come to respect one another and we share in the almost daily new achievements that Sean is now demonstrating and marvel at how wrong the doctors had been in his prognosis.

In recent months, Marie has come to admit to me that she felt there could one day be a medical explanation for his injury and that hopefully we will be able to finally have a cause, so that we need not constantly worry about it happening again. I agree with her that there is always a small nagging doubt every time Sean bangs his head or has a fall. It had become so obvious to Sean that, even when he was on the opposite side of the room, if you told him off for his behaviour he would clutch his head and say 'ouch!' knowing that the whole family was paranoid about him injuring his head.

Marie and I share a love of children and she has, on occasion, mentioned her own sons. I can tell that had we met in other circumstances there would have been no doubt that we could have been close friends. She is a woman who is well read and she often refers to mistakes and miscarriages of justice in history. Together we debate how they might have been avoided only to conclude that sometimes only more research and the passing of time brings such things to light. I make a mental note to read some of the books she talks of, interested in learning more about some of the cases.

As I place the letter on the kitchen worktop I smile at Mark who has come to show me his latest masterpiece. It is first thing in the morning and the weather is fine. I consider taking the children to the park as Sean, now tottering at high speed, comes into the kitchen to join his brother, shaking a tambourine.

My attention drifts almost subconsciously back to the letter again and I re-read it, pondering on how such a long battle could end with a simple letter. That was it. No more visits and no more meetings. I felt cheated. I was almost angry that after all the time I had spent with Marie she hadn't said goodbye, but as I read the letter again it dawns on me that she had planned to call one last time the previous Tuesday and now, a couple of days later, she was legally unable to do so as the order had expired.

I think for a few moments and having recently passed my driving test, at the grand old age of twenty seven, I now muse on the idea of going to say goodbye myself. The thought is a little daunting, I don't even know where the Social Services offices are, they are over half an hours drive away on some very narrow and twisty roads and who is to know if she is even there.

I pick up the phone and dial the number for her office, as I have so often done. I know the number off by heart and, as the call is answered, I ask to speak to Marie, only to be told she is not in the office that day. As I tell the receptionist who I am, I hear her repeat the information to someone standing nearby.

Within seconds I hear the voice of Marie's line manager Andrea. "Hi Heather, it's Andrea. I can get Marie for you if you like, it's her last day and we are going to be having a bit of an office party. We are just fielding calls for her." I giggle as I can now clearly make out the bantering and happy chatter from Marie's colleagues. I don't know why I feel the need, but my mouth makes the decision for me, "Can I call in? I want the boys to say goodbye?" Andrea readily agrees to the request and immediately speaks of how pleased Marie will be to see them and say farewell. I go to hang up the phone and then quickly add: "Andrea? Don't tell her were coming."

I get in the car, still unsure why I feel the need to pay a visit to a social worker of all people. Our lives would never be the same again and the paranoia of what had happened was far reaching. It would change the way some of my friends brought up their children; it made people we knew change their working practices; and it made my family realise that the system doesn't always protect you.

Today though was different. Marie wasn't the system; she was a friend, someone I had come to trust. Mark and Sean were never told why Marie visited and they had come to accept it as normal. I imagined them wondering why she never came to see them anymore having been so involved. Of course the visits had slowly tailed off, but we had seen less of most of our family than of the social worker in the last two and a half years. It seems right somehow that we should say goodbye.

As I arrive somewhere near to where I think the offices are, I ask for directions and park in a nearby street. I am sure there is parking at the offices but I am still new to this whole driving thing and so I park on a side street nearby for an easy get-away. I walk up to the building and find the reception.

Having never been in these particular offices I look around, seeing little Union Jack flags everywhere, clearly for some kind of event and then balloons, which I assume must be for Marie. I walk up to the front desk and announce to the receptionist who I am as a face appears behind her. Andrea, Marie's line manager, was the woman I had first spoken to at Social Services. Her very short, cropped hair is still feminine and her face is all smiles as she tells me she will fetch Marie.

I hover in the entrance uncertainly, not sure what I will say other than goodbye, but as the children stand one either side of me, I see the receptionist's admiring gaze and I know that Marie has helped me to keep them. The security doors swing open and as Marie takes in the three people standing in front of her I see her hand shoot to her mouth accompanied by a gasp.

Marie is a very reserved woman, who wears practical clothes and sensible shoes and likes the outdoors. She looks self-conscious and red in the face with embarrassment, but delighted all the same. She looks around to request approval for bringing us through into the main offices but then decides that she will bring us through anyway, commenting that they could hardly sack her now. I smile, pleased that I have made the effort and happy to feel included in the occasion, albeit having gate-crashed it.

Marie introduces the children to various members of staff that I have never met, I get the strong impression that both Mark and Sean are well known in the office and the case had probably been discussed openly and at length. We walk past the end of several desks, all with nibbles on which are soon offered to the boys who accept keenly. Bowled over by their sudden notoriety they explore their surroundings.

I hang back a little, not wanting to interfere, knowing that perhaps there are confidential records or notes that I shouldn't see. I have no reason or inclination to pry into the lives of others; I know what it was like to feel under siege. I keep a discrete distance and refuse the offer of a chair.

I had only wanted to have the opportunity to thank Marie for her support, to have the chance to say goodbye. I want to end things properly and I feel awkward, right up until something hits me like a lightening bolt.

Marie chats to the boys continually, introducing them to people, handing them snacks, explaining the workings of the office and showing them her desk. It is here that the reason for my visit was made clear to me. Glancing at the working desk of a social worker who had, it seemed, stormed into our lives, who had spent so many hours with me and my children, I see something that draws my eye.

Next to Marie's desk is a wall of pictures and postcards from destinations she has been to, wants to visit or that friends have sent. In the middle of the collage is a picture I recognise instantaneously. Mark and Sean's beaming smiles stand out against the backdrop of locations and scenery as their faces, so familiar to me, jump out. I knew then why I had gone the extra mile; it was because she had gone the extra mile. We would never lose the lasting bond that we had shared; we had forged an understanding, even a friendship, in adversity and for the benefit of the children...my children.

Marie shows me into a side room where we talk briefly and I thank her for her support. She returns the favour by stating we should never have been put in the situation we had found ourselves in. I understand that she has always had a job to do and we had sometimes argued over the need for her to do it, me insisting that we were capable parents and her insisting that Social Services must follow up on all accusations of abuse.

We chat amicably as Marie shows me a photo of her new granddaughter and I exclaim how cute she is and consider how her parents might have coped if their world had been disrupted and turned upside down like ours had. I can tell that the same thought had occurred to her as she reiterates that it should never have happened to us. There are no longer any angry feelings towards Marie, those I reserved for the experts paid in silver for their reports.

The conversation comes to a natural end and I get up to leave, asking the boys if they will give Marie a goodbye cuddle. They both oblige and I smile as the tables are turned and for the first time it is Marie's eyes that are the ones that water. She exits the room in an attempt to recover her composure and disassembles the office decorations to give to the boys.

I wave her goodbye one last time and Mark and Sean wave twice as hard. We both feel we were at the closing stages of a long journey, but as I head out into the sunshine, glad I have made the effort, I laugh: "Now all I've got to do lads is to find where I parked the car!"

CHAPTER 29.

It is several years now since I have seen Marie and life is calm. Sean will always have an issue with easy bruising and prolonged bleeding and only this week a letter has come asking for Mark to go for testing. My experience has taught me never to take my children for granted. Like all mums I sometimes wish for a little more peace and quiet, a bit more time to read a book or a lot less ironing, but I am thankful.

My sons are a joy, easy going in nature, lively, intelligent and good looking (even if I do say so myself). I am of course completely biased and have no problem admitting so. I still marvel at how they can get along together, a fact that will never cease to amaze me until my dying day.

My brother and I are only eighteen months apart in age and yet we fought non stop, calling a truce only if we were on holiday or staying at either of my Grandma's houses. For his part my elder brother is a self-confessed wind-up merchant, who loves nothing better than to get a reaction out of someone. He is an incessant cheat, who firmly holds with the theory that rules are there to be broken. I spent most of my childhood believing that I was rubbish at all board games and jigsaws, only to find that he used to move the counters and nick the pieces.

That said I am proud of him, proud that he serves his country in the army and I share in the worry when he gets posted to a war zone. I would go to the ends of the earth for him now as an adult - if only to push him off! (Only joking mate, honest.) In all we are a normal family, we laugh together, cry together, stand by each other and with each other but we will never forget what could so easily have been.

We could have lost our children to a care system that statistics show let these children down. Their chances of obtaining a good education would have dropped dramatically as so often, children in care are moved to many different homes and different schools. Our children could have ended up in the criminal law system with over twenty-five percent of prisoners having been in care as children. At the age of only sixteen they would have been expected to live independently as adults, without the fallback of a loving home and parents to support them.

Disenfranchised youngsters in our society often have their roots in care, they are less likely to find work due to prejudice or previous behaviour and no matter how good a foster parent or care worker is, they can never replace the need for a child to 'belong', to be part of a family and to be accepted for who they are. That said, a child in care is still better off than any number of children who are regularly abused. We must all aim to protect every child and aim to get it right every time.

In writing this book I never wanted to point the finger. I never wanted people to feel sorry for us, we are the lucky ones. We have our children and we are being allowed to bring them up. I wanted to tell my story, to expose major failings and I wanted people to stop the blind faith they have that the system will prevail. It seems ludicrous, in view of the fact that cases such as Victoria Climbié and Baby P come to light, proving that the guilty are often not caught until it is too late, to assume that the innocent are always proved so in the end.

The aforementioned cases also highlight why the work of our social system is so important. We need to allow professionals to act within their capacity. Multi-agency working is only useful if all the agencies have an equal say. Case conferences are pointless exercises in giving the appearance of sharing information and opinion, when the outcome is pre-ordained and the other agency representatives are ignored.

We were able to find the cause of Sean's bleeding problems only because of his epilepsy, a chance nosebleed and a willingness of those involved to listen. Without the persistence of the haematologists who took over his case, and who determinedly sought to find the cause, we may never have known what had happened.

We could have lost both our children to a system that protects the perceived welfare of the child by following 'expert' medical opinion blindly. Indeed, despite the fact that Mark was a happy and unusually bright child, he and his brother could have been taken into a care system that is known for turning out maladjusted youths by failing to provide stable homes and relying on the amazing work of far too few foster carers, put under immense pressure by the system.

Our care system relies on providing practical placements for children but beds and toys do not make a home. I have worked with some of the most challenging young adults and I know how the system provides recipes for dealing with a variety of situations, despite the fact that the situations and the people in them are vastly different.

I witnessed the damage done to a young lad, whose sisters had been sexually abused by their father. All three children were taken into care but the brother was not allowed to be placed with his sisters due to the risk of him abusing them. His mother had stood by her husband and so none of the children were allowed to see their parents. The young lad felt betrayed by the mother who had put her husband first and felt lost, as his contact with his sisters had become spasmodic, not least because the homes they had been placed in were so far apart. The system set the rules to protect the girls from further abuse but thought nothing about what their brother was experiencing.

I have often wondered how the doctors who write these reports feel about the job they do. Upon talking to the paediatricians I have met, I realise that they are 'sold' a version of what happens to parents like us. They are told that they must follow the flow chart and if the possibility (note the word *possibility*) of an injury being inflicted rather than acquired is raised, they must report it.

The system, whilst crude in its simplicity, fails to acknowledge the considerable intelligence of the medical professionals in making an initial assessment of the situation in front of them. Even that isn't the real failure in this scenario. The doctors are led to believe that if they raise the possibility of non-accidental injury, Social Services will investigate and assess whether or not the injury was likely to have been inflicted.

Doctors write reports safe in the knowledge that the system will protect the innocent. What they do not know and what the system does not take account of, is that if no reason can be found, the parents are left playing a dangerous game of 'fill in the blanks'. Social workers can't walk away from a suspected non-accidental injury once it has been documented on a report and therefore, unless you can explain it, you will end up in the court system. It becomes a circular argument, with doctors reporting possible injuries, expecting social workers to investigate and decide the cause and social workers waving medical reports at parents and stating that they know the cause and have to act.

There are issues which desperately need addressing, such as why it is that when doctors normally diagnose conditions, they are allowed in the case of non-accidental injury to diagnose the cause? Liver problems are not solely linked to alcohol; people who never smoke unfortunately get cancer; those who have broken limbs have not necessarily been in a fight. Why is it then that in cases of Shaken Baby Syndrome or N.A.I. doctors are asked for the cause rather than simply a diagnosis?

It would be perfectly acceptable for medical professionals to state a possible list of causes but they cannot state so definitively which one is correct. Unfortunately some doctors seem to insist that injuries are abusive and offer mathematical likelihood as the reason for their conviction.

The first doctor to see Sean's scan's, Dr. Fieldman, was later to be involved in the case of another mother and father, who aborted the child they were expecting at the time of the trial, as they could not face the possibility of a second child being taken. Many people do not realise that any future children parents may have will automatically invoke an investigation by Social Services, even before the child is born and even when the original investigation has ended. The family could simply not cope with any further intrusion and stress.

The cause of the bleed on their son's brain was initially suggested as violent shaking but was later attributed to a lack of oxygen in the womb. The twelve months of hell they endured left lasting emotional scars and had led to the abortion of a much wanted sibling for their son, who was eventually returned to them. The couple however, could not undo the abortion of their second baby or the damage it left behind.

These types of cases are legion and they read like a constant list of flawed science and accusations without evidence, as medical opinion slowly replaces the need for facts, reason or justice. How many more parents must endure trial by expert before there will be more investment in the research needed to correctly diagnose our children?

The fact that some doctors are paid to write reports on children they have never seen is surely bad practice. Sean never saw the doctor who wrote the report that landed us in court and the County Council's legal team refused to disclose who had instructed the doctor in question to offer an opinion. The factual inaccuracies in the report raised doubts about whether any of Sean's history had been relayed; I later discovered it had not. Even if it had, it would only raise further issues as to patient confidentiality. We later found out that several hospitals had some of Sean's notes, hospitals that Sean had never attended and never been referred to, begging the question as to why they were in possession of his records.

It would be better practice to ensure that reports to the court are sent from treating physicians, who have the best knowledge of the patient and their medical history. In legal cases, certain individuals become known for their willingness to provide opinions, in return for a fee, their opinions rarely moving from an established standpoint. These individuals become 'regulars' in the family courts, where they are provided with a soap box for their own hypothesis and where the burden of proof is probability, not proven guilt.

The difficulty in almost all of these cases is that parents never get to put their side of the story or get to speak to the experts in the case face to face. We were unable to ask the doctors who wrote the reports about all of the facts we felt were relevant and to establish whether or not they were aware of them. Despite giving suitcase loads of information to our solicitor, virtually none of it got to court. Deals that were struck on our behalf were hidden from us and we were simply the bystanders.

The instructing letter to the neuroradiologist, Dr. Timmins, never came to light and yet research has since shown that in similar cases where the same brain scan was shown to neuroradiologists with different causes inferred by those instructing them, their opinion as to the cause changed. In criminal courts no one is allowed to prejudice the outcome or lead witnesses, but in cases of shaken baby syndrome neuroradiologists are asked if non-accidental injury could be the cause when the report is requested. This surely gives an impression by the party requesting the report that they find this a distinct possibility, thereby prejudicing the doctor's opinion before the report is even written.

As parents are continually prevented from speaking out about their experiences, both by the courts and by the belief that they will be judged by others, it is impossible to determine accurately how many cases of alleged abuse have been later attributed to medical conditions. It is also worth mentioning that in some cases inherited conditions have only come to light after a child has already been placed in the care of the Local Authority.

Some parents, like me, are diagnosed with bleeding conditions themselves leading them to conclude that their children may be at risk. If they no longer have care of their children, the parents are left panic stricken at the idea that their child, wherever they may be, may suffer a major bleed again and that the appropriate tests may never be carried out.

I raise another interesting diagnostic flaw in respect of the ophthalmology reports that were submitted in Sean's case. The courts and the public have often been told of the 'triad' of injuries that is suggestive, or even classed as evidence of, shaken baby syndrome. Why then, when one initial ophthalmologist's report stated that they could find no haemorrhaging in Sean's eyes, was another ophthalmologist even asked to look?

Why did the first specialist not see any haemorrhages but another specialist later report that there were some? Why, if the second specialist observed haemorrhaging that they then attributed to bleeding at birth, did they then write a report stating that non-accidental injury must be excluded and how can it be excluded? If there is no witch hunt against parents why is it that there is a need to repeat tests until the findings fit the alleged diagnosis?

When Mark was six weeks old we were involved in a car crash on the main road, not far ironically from the Stockport Hospital. A young driver had been waved out of a side road by a driver in the slow lane of the A6. Failing to recognize that the other lane of traffic that we were in, was still moving at thirty miles per hour, she pulled in front of us

214

Darron's quick reactions prevented our heavy estate from ploughing into the side of her old mini, as she froze, failing to apply her brakes as Darron swerved as much as he dare.

The resultant crash caused whiplash to me and Mark's car seat flipped completely over as it was designed to do, forming a hard protective shell from the impact. Mark and I were taken to Accident and Emergency but were soon discharged, me with pain killers and Mark with a quick once over and a reference to the fact that babies are resilient.

Mark was later found to have retinal haemorrhaging and bruising but he never saw an ophthalmologist at the hospital after the crash and he never had a brain scan. How can a doctor state that a car crash is similar to the force required to recreate the findings in shaken baby cases, if when car crashes occur they don't investigate? Why is it acceptable to ask an ophthalmologist to look at a baby in order to try and prove potential abuse but fail to do so when checking a baby for injury in a proven accidental situation? These questions not only need to be asked, they need to be answered.

CHAPTER 30.

Luck seems to play such a large part in these types of cases. I had a lot of time for the social worker who eventually saw us home but no time at all for the initial case worker who was prepared to pressurise and lie in order to get to an answer, regardless of whether the answer was right or wrong. In defence of all social workers they have high case loads and high stress levels. They are never welcome in cases of child protection and yet they have to try and remain impartial until the assessments are complete.

It would be unheard of for a police officer to be dispatched to deal with a violent criminal alone, yet social workers are often sent in to the homes of potentially violent individuals, where they could be at great risk.. In cases where child abuse is suspected, particularly violence against a child, it is reasonable to assume that a lone person, quite often female, would be at risk. This would lead any person to try to protect themselves and possibly to tread lightly.

This could lead to a failure in assessing these types of situations and protecting children. Who hasn't had to make a telephone call or visit they haven't wanted to make and been happy to find the person doesn't answer. It allows us to justify to ourselves that we tried and to happily move on to something else.

It is also interesting to note that initially we were emotionally blackmailed into naming which of us was the perpetrator. I knew neither of us would have injured Sean and therefore I was convinced that there must be a medical explanation, but had our marriage not been as strong what would have happened then? It would be all too easy for a separated parent to accuse the other or suggest that an ex-partner had injured the child.

Whilst these cases are bad enough, what if the courts made an order forbidding access to the child or, even worse, if a guilty parent successfully managed to convince social workers of their partner's guilt? It is vital that social workers look at each case and assess the situation for themselves. It is also important that if they can find no reason for abuse and no further evidence of abuse they are able to make the decision to close a case without fear of reprisal.

We can't possibly trust a social worker implicitly when they report abuse and rush to take children into care and yet not trust them to be capable of deciding that a case does not warrant further action, despite non-accidental injury being raised as a possible cause, if there is no evidence.

Social Services must be given the provision to help families. Would it not be easier to have a 'care home' where the whole family can live? A place where assessments can be carried out speedily and in-depth and even where young mums or vulnerable mothers can be given help and respite from the demanding role of motherhood. If we had not had our children with us it would have been much harder to demonstrate our parental skills and in many cases this hinders families being reunited. These provisions exist in some cases but they are under funded and not available to all. If Mark had not been born first and had not proven to be the happy, settled and intelligent child that he is, both children would have been removed, despite the fact that we would have been no guiltier. In these situations once children are removed the parents have no way of proving their worth.

The mental state of parents needs to be considered as a matter of great importance, both at the time an incident is reported and throughout any upcoming case. Any person involved in a lengthy legal battle will be under immense strain, which will only compound any underlying problems. Many men and women in a situation where they feel powerless to help their families will react to professionals in an angry manner.

It is perfectly understandable that parents would fight to protect their children more fiercely than anything else and yet any hint of anger, even controlled anger, is portrayed as a sign of guilt and used against parents in reports and assessments. Obviously, any show of violence is completely unacceptable but professionals need to be aware that anger at being in the situation is a normal reaction and that it does not necessarily indicate that a person is normally aggressive.

In my opinion there also needs to be a system in place to exonerate parents if a medical cause for the alleged abuse is discovered. When I telephoned the Social Services offices and requested information on how to add Sean's diagnosis to his file I was summarily dismissed with the statement, "You've just informed us." After everything we had been through we had no faith in Social Services' record keeping and wanted to ensure that the diagnosis was included in the case file.

The duty social worker continued to tell me that the information wouldn't change the file, as the file recorded the history of the case and could not be amended. I persevered as I was convinced that if a diagnosis is made there must be some way of ensuring this knowledge is included with the documentation of the case. I was told that any letter of diagnosis from a doctor would remain with Sean's file but that we would have to return to court to formally amend the record.

Bearing in mind that the cost to our family alone, in increased living expenses, court costs and the loss of earnings ran into thousands, it seems a further indictment of the system that there is no straight forward way of amending the records. The cost of legal representation and court fees prohibits families from formally amending the cause of any injury, even when there is a medical diagnosis.

The same is also true of the child's medical notes which, in alleged abuse cases, are filled with additional doctors letters and advice relating to the child being classed as 'at risk', information which is potentially also included on the files of any siblings. Trying to have the correct diagnosis made obvious to any treating professionals whilst also ensuring that it replaces the existing accusation, is difficult and costly.

Having also been interviewed by the police in relation to a possible case of child cruelty, the police interview tapes were also held on file. After the police had finished interrogating us I had checked with the police sergeant what would happen to the tapes since we had not been arrested or charged. I was informed that if the case did not proceed to criminal prosecution tapes were destroyed after five years. Therefore, for parents who may have been questioned, arrested or even charged in connection with an alleged non-accidental injury, police records will also exist in connection to the case.

If Mark had also been of school age, the school's Child Protection Officer would also have been included in the meetings that were held and for other families in this situation, so yet another file would exist. The very thing that helps protect children, the sharing of information with all relevant parties, also goes against parents who are attempting to exonerate themselves and formally change the cause of the injury.

I think it is very clear that there should be a simple mechanism for parents to apply to court to have all records changed. It is not only fair but it is also necessary to a child's safety, that medical professionals are aware of any new diagnosis. Frequently when I take Sean to hospital appointments I am asked to paraphrase his notes as they are so extensive that finding relevant information is almost impossible.

The haematologists have done their utmost to highlight his bleeding condition with coloured pages clearly detailing the problem, even going so far as to add post-it notes with reference to it on the initial letters to social services, that are copied on his file. Everyone hates injustice and mistakes will always happen, but when they have happened there needs to be a straight forward way to put them right.

CHAPTER 31.

If you have never had any dealings with the family courts, you would be forgiven for thinking that they are actually a branch of MI5. The mystery and secrecy surrounding the courts are justified to all by the need to protect a child's identity throughout proceedings and I understand this completely. However, this protection does not seem to extend to medical files and other documents. Minutes of meetings, if taken at all, were often distributed haphazardly and frequently copied to professionals we had no dealing with. To this day we have never met or spoken to some of those professionals copied in on letters sent to us.

If secrecy is necessary for reasons of confidentiality there is no reason to keep the workings of the court a mystery. We found it very difficult to get any information about the actual court process. We were never actually advised to get a solicitor and didn't know what options, if any, we had. There was no advice about choosing a solicitor and when we did instruct one, she frequently negotiated without us being aware of what was being agreed to. We were at a loss to understand what Social Services might do or what they were legally allowed to do, believing all threats without question. Even the words 'case conference', 'Guardian' and 'fact finding' were completely new to us and our families.

Obtaining legal representation is of vital importance in any legal case but in family proceedings, when the very heart of your existence, your children, are at stake, there can be nothing more crucial. The difficulties in finding good legal representation are often not apparent to those who have never been in the situation we found ourselves in. Family law is different to criminal law and in care proceedings parents need a specialist solicitor that can handle the intricacies of such a case.

Most high street solicitors are used to dealing with conveyance, divorce or probate, but they are rarely specialists in the complexity of family law. For us the nearest family law firms were over half an hours drive away and with such tight restrictions on our movement it became really difficult to meet with any of them. We were left ringing around firms trying to find out if they had any experience of cases such as ours and ask probing questions to see if they would be the best firm to represent us.

Unfortunately, by the very nature of these accusations and the speed at which a child at risk can be removed from a parents care, parents are left with little time to arrange representation. It is exceptionally difficult when you are under such stress and with very little time, to instruct a carefully chosen solicitor, even if you know what questions to ask.

Most parents I have spoken to simply pick a solicitor who is available when they call, is nearest to their home or who seems approachable and friendly. None of these factors give parents any indication that the solicitor they have chosen is the one who will represent them best and offer the best defence, bringing all the necessary factors before the judge.

Parents frequently have little say in the way their cases are handled and they are often given advice on what course to take based on the outcome of previous cases. Unless you have ever been in the situation it is hard to describe the impossible choice of fighting for what you know to be the truth and risking losing your children and agreeing to accept a version of the proposed facts in order to guarantee that your children will be safely returned to your care.

Even legal teams that represent the parents put so much weight on previous case outcomes that, if your case falls in a minority or you have additional evidence, the advice you will receive will be the same as those of the majority who have gone before. Most cases are fought in exactly the same way with each side using preferred experts and following a set method, limiting the chances of ever getting a different end result.

Most disputed cases will eventually go to 'fact finding', which is the most questionable practice of the family courts. When the parents or carers stand together and fail to point the finger at each other or a third party, there is a need to name the perpetrator. When no direct evidence exists as to who may have inflicted the injury, or even, as in our case, whether there was one, the court seeks to find facts.

These are best guesses as to what happened and who was responsible based on information put before the court, perceived opportunity and possible motive. Local Authority barristers and solicitors suggest the most likely scenario and the use of a psychologist's report to re-enforce the likelihood of that scenario is not unusual. The psychologist in our case, and therefore surely those in other cases, have been known to write reports which are flawed and at times misrepresenting. It seems that this doesn't really matter, once the facts have been found they are now the facts, all based on the assumption that an injury occurred in the first place.

The Guardian in our case was noticeable, mainly, by his spasmodic appearances. When we asked if he would visit the children, as we believed it was part of his role, he joked with his solicitor that if he came he would be able to take instruction from his client. Sean at age one was unable to converse and it was made obvious to us that he was reluctant to make the journey to see us.

Darron and I overheard Isaac saying that he 'failed to see the point' in a visit. Surely anyone appointed by the courts, with such a pivotal role in the future of a family, should at least have observed the family dynamic and the children's welfare? It would be astounding to make a decision without visiting the children. The Guardian was also surprised by our own home surroundings as, even though he was aware of Social Services requests that we live away from home, it hadn't occurred to him that he had never seen our own property.

Once he had made the trip to visit us he remarked at how child-centred and safe our home was, having originally believed my parents' house to be ours. If the Guardian is to represent the interests of a child successfully they must be able to make informed decisions and consider all the environmental factors. It goes to prove the point that the system only works if everyone in the system *works* to make it work.

We were fortunate that with the help of our extended family and having enough knowledge to challenge a significant proportion of the, so called, evidence against us, that we were the first parents in the UK to keep our children with us throughout proceedings of this nature. We managed day after day to make the professionals involved in the case look deeper, question more and ask themselves, "If they could see no reason for us to injure our children, why would we?"

I submitted copious letters and documents, which ran to many pages, which countered the claim of abuse. I read medical journals, learnt about brain scans and their limitations and researched possible alternative causes for bleeds on the brain. With all the hours of research and help from those closest to us, I would still never have found the answer if the medical profession had not re-evaluated their opinions and been prepared to investigate further.

Some people might presume that I am angry that the diagnosis did not come sooner, but there is no room for anger when fighting injustice. I am who I am because of what happened. I have learnt to embrace life with ever fibre of my being, to value every moment with my children and revel in their achievements and I know that I can share it all with all my family and our great many friends, who never wavered in their support.

The timing of our case coincided with a huge increase in media coverage of false allegations of shaken baby syndrome, making those professionals involved in our case more wary of treading the same path and giving hope to the considerable numbers of parents who were trying to prove their innocence.

In July of 2005, one month after the end of our case, the court of Appeals in the UK reversed or reduced three convictions of shaken baby syndrome, finding that the triad of retinal haemorrhage, subdural haematoma and acute brain swelling are not necessarily diagnostic and that clinical history is also important.

The term non-accidental trauma is now used instead of shaken baby syndrome, the latter now being so commonly associated with miscarriages of justice. The medical profession will never help to obtain justice for all if they rename a syndrome instead of looking deeper at the medical findings connected with it.

It is no longer enough to be eminent, children all over the UK are being taken away from their parents and even if only five percent of babies are incorrectly diagnosed and five percent of parents wrongly accused then it is still five percent too many.

About the Author

Heather Toomey grew up and now resides in Buxton, Derbyshire, an idyllic location in the Peak District, known for its mineral water. She works as an IT Network Manager for a local school and she enjoys playing and listening to music, dancing and spending time with her family.

She lives with her motorbike obsessed husband, Darron and her two children Mark and Sean. The eldest, Mark, being more of a natural writer than she ever was and her youngest, Sean, who is so energetic it tires you out watching him. Her West Highland Terrier, Mac, is never far behind any of them and especially close when food is on offer!

She has written this book to raise awareness of the number of families accused of abusing their child by shaking; unproven accusations, that are difficult to bear and impossible to defend.

12614489R00134

Printed in Great Britain
by Amazon.co.uk, Ltd.,
Marston Gate.